MW00831071

Borders and Belonging: A Memoir

Mira Sucharov

Borders and Belonging: A Memoir

palgrave
macmillan

Mira Sucharov
Ottawa, ON, Canada

ISBN 978-3-030-53731-9   ISBN 978-3-030-53732-6   (eBook)
https://doi.org/10.1007/978-3-030-53732-6

This Palgrave Macmillan imprint is published by the registered company Springer Nature Switzerland AG
The registered company address is: Gewerbestrasse 11, 6330 Cham, Switzerland

ACKNOWLEDGMENTS

I am grateful to the many friends, family, and colleagues who made this work possible.

Thank you to Anca Pusca for her editorial vision, and to Geetha Chockalingam and the rest of the production team at Palgrave Macmillan. Anca's commitment to memoir as representing a legitimate form of scholarly publishing is a model for academic editors.

With patience and insight, Shulem Deen and Alison Pick taught me how to write memoir. Ayelet Tsabari offered early helpful guidance as well. Polly Rosenwaike provided smart and essential line editing in the latter stages of the project.

Thank you to friends and colleagues who read all or parts of the manuscript and offered feedback at various points along the way: Selina Alko, Jodi Eichler-Levine, Mya Guarnieri Jaradat, Rebecca Katz, Leslie Morris, Alisa Postner, Jerry Ritt, Erica Sher, Martin Shuster, Gila Silverman, Carrie Standil, and Lior Zaltzman. In addition to reading drafts, Hershey Kagan offered generous design consultations. The participants at the narrative writing seminar at the 2018 Association for Jewish Studies conference—including Angela Botelho, Maria Damon, Marc Dollinger, Jodi Eichler-Levine, Aaron Hahn Tapper, Adeena Karasick, Laura Limonic, and Leslie Morris—provided a collaborative space in which to workshop a chapter from this book. Conversations with Laura Levitt, Oded Löwenheim, and Yonit Shemesh enriched the project at key intervals. Thank you to my parents: My dad, Max Sucharov, who was an enthusiastic reader of draft chapters, as well as my mom, Faye Margolis, and my stepmom, Rebecca Toolan, who have been encouraging of the project—and all of my writings—from the outset. My stepdad, Ron Campbell, died, sadly, while the manuscript was nearing completion.

Endless gratitude to my wonderful spouse, Steve, and to our two awesome kids. The continued love, support, good humor, and inspiration I get from all three of you mean everything.

A handful of books and articles are quoted from or mentioned directly. In Chapter 1, I discuss Oded Löwenheim, *The Politics of the Trail: Reflexive Mountain Biking along the Frontier of Jerusalem* (Ann Arbor: University of Michigan Press, 2014); Oded Löwenheim, "The 'I' in IR: An Autoethnographic Account," *International Studies Review* 36, 4 (October 2010): 1023–1045; Oded Löwenheim, "Back to Hebron's Tegart Fort: An Autoethnography of Shame, Love, Loss, and the De-Securitization of the Self," *Journal of Narrative Politics* 1, 2 (Spring 2015). In Chapter 12, I quote from Laura Levitt, *American Jewish Loss After the* Holocaust (New York: New York University Press, 2007), p. 21. In Chapter 13, I make reference to Aaron J. Hahn Tapper and Mira Sucharov, eds., *Social Justice and Israel/Palestine: Foundational and Contemporary Debates* (Toronto: University of Toronto Press, 2019). In Chapter 14, I quote from Alex Rose, "Panel about Jews on Campus Postponed over Security Concerns," *The Canadian Jewish News* (3 January 2020).

Thank you to my colleagues in the department of political science at Carleton University who have created a supportive space to write, teach and create. The Faculty of Public Affairs at Carleton provided generous funding to support the final stages of preparing the manuscript. Finally, I am grateful to my lively social media network for many passionate conversations about Israel-Palestine and Jewish politics, conversations that have shaped me emotionally, politically and intellectually. All errors or omissions are mine alone.

Ottawa, Canada   Mira Sucharov
April 2020

Author's Note

This is a work of memoir. All events are as I remember them. Dialogue is reconstructed from memory or else has been re-created in approximate ways, following the conventions of the genre. I have consulted the historical record as needed to ensure accuracy around publicly-recorded events. With the exception of direct family members, unless first and last names are used together, all names have been changed.

PROLOGUE

"Sorry, Mira," the email says, "I need to pull out of the group. My husband doesn't want you in our home."

I swallow hard. The email is from a woman I know from the local Jewish community. Years ago, we had spent the afternoon together in her tidy suburban home, surrounded by dress-up clothes and dollhouses, as our daughters played noisily.

A few weeks earlier, I had created a Bar and Bat Mitzvah project group for Jewish youth around town. My daughter's Bat Mitzvah was coming up, and I wanted to shore up the Ottawa cohort. Create a sense of community. Encourage families to see how this personal milestone could be mobilized to pursue a smattering of social justice.

We, the parents, had spent a week over email coordinating the timing and locations and guest list and program and menu. Rotating hosts would supply the space and the refreshments, and I promised to guide the kids in designing a social justice campaign on a topic of their choice. First we'd learn how to identify wrongs that need righting. I figured I would start with something simple. A fictional scenario about a jelly bean factory in crisis, maybe. I'd ask the kids to consider why the factory had suddenly run out of jelly beans. What might the causes and remedies be? We'd talk about justice. We'd think about individuals and structures and systems. The workers' conditions. The children who needed the jelly beans. The price of sugar. The town's water supply.

Once we identified causes and solutions, we'd consider how to leverage social media to help repair the world. We'd learn about Maimonides's ethical ladder of charity. And I'd try my best, I promised myself, to keep my own politics out of it. Mostly, anyway. I'd encourage the kids to come to their own conclusions. And at the end of the evening, we'd eat ice cream and drink hot cocoa. "Hot Chocolate for Hot Issues," I called it.

I continue reading the woman's email. "My husband says you support a group calling for the destruction of Israel and the Jewish people."

My mind spins. Which group is her husband thinking of? It can't be the local Jewish community boards I've sat on. Those are each squarely mainstream, though I've admittedly tried to push their boundaries. Maybe it's the American Jewish organization I'm on the board of, and for which I fundraise and travel to New York once a year for meetings. For that group, I've been working to get a progressive slate elected to the World Zionist Organization. The group is certainly liberal, but it's definitely Zionist, so it can't be that one. And would he even know about it? Or maybe it's the academic group I'm part of, the one that tries to oppose the occupation *and* oppose attempts at boycotting Israeli academia. That one is also liberal, but also within the Zionist consensus. And it's against BDS—Boycott, Divestment, and Sanctions against Israel—after all.

So, with my cheeks burning, I ask her: "Which group would that be?"

I wait for half an hour, irritated and restless, before a reply arrives in my inbox.

"The Palestinian people in general."

And then she links to an article, an op-ed I'd recently published. My editor at the *Globe and Mail* had titled it "The problem with picking sides in the Israeli-Palestinian conflict." In that piece, I was trying to lay out what I saw as a balanced approach for my Canadian readers.

A few years later, it's true, I would come to question even that sort of approach. I would come to advance a more justice-forward, elbows-out position: clearly not the direction her husband would want. But my stance is measured in this *Globe and Mail* piece she's sent me.

Measured is clearly not good enough for them. "As an Israel supporter," she writes, "there is only one side."

I close my email program and, with teeth clenched, open a Facebook window.

"Wow. A new personal low for internal Jewish communal relations," I write, as I describe what happened, with the incident scrubbed of names.

Reactions start to roll in.

"You'd be invited into my house and asked to stay for dinner!"

"Don't be afraid to keep talking . . . eventually they will hear you."

"I am deeply ashamed of my Jewish community."

"Time for this woman to stand up for herself!"

I'm grateful for the solidarity, and I click "like."

A few minutes later, a friendly acquaintance calls about some other matter. I fill her in on what I've been going through today. But I don't get the reaction I'm hoping for. "If you're gonna put yourself out there, you're gonna get burned," she says.

And for the rest of the day, all I have is my righteous indignation and a splitting headache. How did I come to be perceived, by those who seemingly liked me enough to chat every day at pickup time outside of the JCC preschool and to smile across the room at baby music classes and to invite me to their home for playdates, as an enemy of the Jews?

And some years later, how did I come to not often even know *what* I believed? How did my political and ethical rudder—once so firm and certain—start to warp from the waters of communal pressures coming at me from all directions?

When it comes to the topic of Israel—a subject on which I was suckled and weaned during seven years of Jewish day school, a decade at Hebrew summer camp, and three years living in the country, soaking up the atmosphere and sometimes dreaming about moving there myself—when it comes to Israel, a subject on which I have claimed to be a scholar-specialist for all of my adult life, and about which I have never hesitated in speaking up and speaking out, I guess I should have known that anything is possible.

CONTENTS

CHAPTER 1

Posters & Flags

2011

I've arrived at Rabin Square, in central Tel Aviv, half an hour early.

The year I lived in Tel Aviv, in the mid-nineties, the square was called *Malchei Israel*, Kings of Israel. That April during the Passover holiday, I had dragged myself out of my apartment near trendy Sheinkin Avenue, walked across town, and traversed the square to see the latest Woody Allen movie as my roommates traveled for the holiday and the city streets were eerily quiet.

Four months after I returned to Canada to begin a Master's degree, Prime Minister Yitzhak Rabin was gunned down by a right-wing Israeli extremist. That afternoon, I spoke for hours on the phone with Steve, the boyfriend who would later become my husband; he at his parents' house in Vancouver, and I in my apartment in downtown Toronto. As my roommate and I shifted our house party planned for that night to an impromptu vigil, we tried to absorb the hateful politics of it all. That night, we all sat on hand-me-down furniture and watched CBC news on our small TV until late. Soon after, the Tel Aviv square was renamed in Rabin's honor.

Tonight there is a buzz in the air. Clusters of men and women, my age or younger, are milling about. Some are wearing baby slings; others are holding signs and cigarettes. All are dressed casually: in jeans, shorts, sandals, or sneakers. The sun is starting to set, taking the edge off the stifling June heat.

© The Author(s) 2021
M. Sucharov, *Borders and Belonging: A Memoir*,
https://doi.org/10.1007/978-3-030-53732-6_1

A few days earlier, I'd seen a peace march advertised on Facebook. "Will you be there?" I asked Omri. He, a fellow scholar in my field, and his wife Abigail, another academic, had generously offered to host me for a few days in their apartment so I could continue the research trip I had planned.

Steve and our two kids had left Israel a few days earlier and returned to Ottawa, after a family trip where we traversed the country in our rental car and fought locals for parking spots, sipped frozen *nana* lemonade at the local cafe, let the fish nibble our toes in the Sachna pools, watched the falafel guy in Afula toss crunchy chickpea balls high into the air before catching them in a waiting pita pocket, and tracked a turtle in the desert while our four-year-old son's hat flew off his head into the hot wind.

We had visited my kibbutz family on their kibbutz a kilometre from the Gaza border, where my "kibbutz dad" had set up a splash pad for our kids in his front yard. We had visited the *shuk* in the town of Sderot, the one that is so often in the news when Hamas launches rockets into Israel's southern area. There, our mind wandered from threats and bomb shelters as we loaded fresh strawberries into a pink plastic bag and picked out a blue and white knitted kippa for my son. We visited my aunt and uncle in the north, where we adults drank homemade limoncello with lemons from their trees as my daughter played snakes and ladders, and I stared across the Green Line toward the Palestinian village of Jenin.

We'd passed by the apartment my husband and I shared the first year we were married, when I was doing research for my dissertation, and that year we would walk every week through the sun and rain to a local pottery studio where we took classes, before stopping at the *makolet* to buy rugelach and returning to our apartment to sip mint tea and watch *Ally McBeal* with Hebrew subtitles. We'd bargained with the vendors in the Jerusalem *shuk* and bought tiny keychains with our kids' Hebrew names. We'd gone to the Kotel, where my seven-year-old daughter balked at the gender segregation and I promised her we'd donate to Women of the Wall. And on the day I gave a talk at Tel Aviv University, my husband had driven the kids across the length of the country to visit his cousin in Haifa, who gave our son and daughter two ice cream cones each: one for each hand.

"Yeah, we'll come to the march," Omri said. "We'll put the baby in the stroller and we can all walk over from our apartment together."

But the rush of domestic life got in the way of them attending. So I'm here on my own, and the march helps distract me. I usually enjoy the thrill of traveling alone. But when I bid Steve and our kids farewell, with another week ahead of me, I feel a sudden curtain of sadness.

I'd once thought I might settle in Israel. It would just be a matter of activating the legal right I have to immigrate, as a Jew, under Israel's Law of Return. Spending weekends on a kibbutz in the northern Negev with my "kibbutz family" in my young twenties, the family that each of us, in our youth group, were assigned for the year as we spent weekends in the small desert community while studying at Hebrew University during the week, helped me picture my own possible adult life in the country. That, and my own extended family, including an aunt and uncle who had made aliya from Winnipeg in the early seventies, and distant cousins who had been here for generations, made it seem possible. Once I met my Canadian Jewish husband and discovered he had a dozen Israeli cousins—relatives on his father's side who had settled in Israel from Romania in the late 40s, as Europe was rebuilding and Israel was being born, the circle felt even more complete.

Experiencing the country again, as a parent now—even for a short couple of weeks, with my kids hearing Hebrew from the mouths of others, and not only from mine like they are used to in Canada where I speak only Hebrew to them, left me wanting more. That afternoon, after Steve and the kids left in a taxi for the airport, I wandered with Omri through a pocket of the redesigned neighborhood of south Tel Aviv, thinking to myself that my kids would have enjoyed riding the stuffed horses on wheels dotting the public courtyard.

The slogans on the signs around me remind me why I'm here. *Peace Now. Jews and Arabs Refuse to Be Enemies. End the Occupation.* And the signs of political parties, the ones on the left end of the Israeli political spectrum: *Meretz. Hadash.* Tonight I'm marching for peace, just like I'd be doing if I were a regular Israeli, my kids in tow, handing them a bag of Bamba, the peanut-butter-flavored snack food, as a reward for their patience. But I'm also reminded that I'm not actually Israeli.

I can recite many of the names of the members of Knesset who occupy the party lists, and my younger cousin is hoping to run for one of those parties in the next election, and I even spent a few months years ago interning in the Knesset—but I have no vote. Still, I feel attached and invested. And I want my voice to matter.

Unlike at Israeli marches of this sort, where "peace" is one of the central demands, the campus activism signs I see back home rarely include the word peace. It's even become a dirty word in some circles. When I was growing up in the Jewish community in Western Canada we sang all manner of Hebrew songs about peace. "Shalom al Yisrael" (Peace upon Israel), "Shir la Shalom" (Song for Peace), "Nolad'ti la'shalom" (I was Born for Peace). But some Palestine solidarity activists these days say that calling for peace is simply a way of whitewashing the Palestinian experience. They say that calling for peace is like demanding that an enslaved person remain quiet in their shackles. Solidarity, anti-oppression, anti-racism, resistance, *summud*—steadfastness in the face of Israeli aggression: to these Palestine solidarity activists, those are the words that matter.

But peace is the word that still animates the Israeli left—or whatever is left of it—so tonight I embrace it, alongside the crowd that has gathered. I'll code-switch as needed, choosing the right words for the right audience. Or at least I'll try to.

A young man shouts into a megaphone and the crowd tightens. My early arrival means I've secured a spot near the front. A young woman to my right hands me a slim pole. I glance upwards along the wooden shaft and see the familiar Israeli peace flag. It resembles the blue and white Israeli flag, but instead of the Star of David is the word Shalom, in Hebrew letters. I nod to her and grasp the flag with a sense of purpose. Soon we are advancing, a throng of dozens and then hundreds, and then eventually a few thousand, down Ibn Gvirol street. I realize I am among those leading the charge, waving my flag.

Through the megaphone come Hebrew chants. They remind me of my decade at Hebrew summer camp, with our team songs and cheers accompanying our marching. "*Plugateinu, yesh lanu ruach … !*" (Our team, we've got spirit!). A pang of longing shoots through me, as it always does when I recall my years at Hebrew summer camp. The intensity of the nostalgia soon gives way to a jolt of electricity as I embrace the moment of being surrounded by Israelis speaking Hebrew. I am partly *of* the group and partly not.

It doesn't take long for the chants to turn salty: "Sara, tell Bibi you won't fuck him until he stops fucking up the country!"

I alternate between chanting without moving my lips and moving my lips without chanting. I'm a little uncomfortable using swear words in Hebrew around Israelis. Partly it's my Canadian accent that I try hard to mask with my best rolled R's. But my general uneasiness goes deeper. It's a citizen's protest, and yet I know very well that while I feel highly attached to Israel, speak only Hebrew to my kids, and listen to Israeli vintage rock music when I need a pick-me-up, I am not a citizen. I have no vote in this protest against the government that represents everyone else here.

When the media announces the numbers, will I be compromising the data? If they report that five thousand people marched for peace, will I need to raise my hand—write a letter to the editor, post on social media—to issue a correction? *Um, not 5,000 citizens. 4,999, actually.*

And if the news cameras were to pan over to me marching, and if my Israeli relatives were to see me on the evening news, would they confront me? *How dare you challenge our government to take actions that affect us, that jeopardize our security, we, who actually live here, while you sit comfortably in your Canadian city, working in the Canadian university where you don't have to have your bag checked by security guards when you enter your campus, you who are raising Canadian children who won't ever have to be drafted? You, who already live in peace?*

Of course, they wouldn't actually *say* "how dare you." They'd ask me quietly probing questions, under the guise of just wanting *to understand.*

Fifteen years ago, I was at my aunt and uncle's house on their kibbutz, visiting for the weekend. That year, I was living with friends in Tel Aviv. To help bankroll my nine months in the country between university degrees, I was conducting research for two professors back in Canada. One of the projects entailed interviewing European officials and Palestinian officials about the political economy of Palestinian state-building. Since I had no office of my own—I used my apartment telephone and public pay phones along the way to make appointments—I had given out my aunt's fax number for the times I needed to receive documents.

One evening, as I was preparing for bed, my aunt said, "There's something we'd like to talk to you about." She was holding a shiny piece of paper. It looked like a fax.

I felt my cheeks get hot.

"We got this today. It says it's from the Palestinian National Authority. And your name is on it." Her voice rose. "Have you been giving my fax number to the PLO?"

"Oh, that." I looked at it and saw that it was some follow-up information from an interview I'd done with a Palestinian official over mint tea at the American Colony Hotel in East Jerusalem.

"I'm doing research for a professor back in Canada," I explained. "I, uh, have to interview political figures about the political economy of the emerging Palestinian government, since the peace deal was signed. Sometimes I interview European diplomats. And sometimes I interview Palestinian officials too. It's just research. I gave out your fax number. I hope that's okay." I looked away.

"We don't want our fax machine used for this. We could get in trouble."

"What kind of trouble?"

"The government, you know." She trailed off.

I silently calculated whether to engage in political debate with her or just apologize for the fax and get the matter over with.

"Sorry. About the fax. I don't have a machine of my own so I thought …" My heart was pounding.

"The fax is one thing," my aunt says. "But what we really want to know is, whose side are you on?"

I knew they were thinking not only about my research interests, my plans to continue on to graduate school to study Israeli–Palestinian relations. I knew they were thinking about Jabir. They hadn't met him, but they had heard about him from my mom. Jabir, a fellow student at McGill in Montreal, was Arab. He'd recently broken up with me—a decision, he had explained in a letter he'd written to me in Vancouver, that was spurred by political pressure from his friends and colleagues. I was still feeling heartbroken.

Whose side are you on?

Sucking in a deep breath, I said, "I'm on the side of peace."

"Peace. Wouldn't that be nice," my uncle said. "We all want peace. But this is a tough neighborhood. Peace won't come until *they* accept *our* right to *exist*."

"But Rabin and Arafat exchanged mutual letters of recognition," I said. "I even cut the letters out of the newspaper and scotch-taped them to my wall last year in —."

My uncle interrupted me. "Do you really think those letters are worth the paper they're written on?"

"Well, they were written under the watch of the international community. Reputation matters," I said. I was invoking concepts I'd learned in my international relations courses. Too dry, I figured. So I tried another tack. "Peace with the Palestinians is gonna help everyone. And part of making peace is to make sure the Palestinians are in good financial shape. They need to create a state, and that means getting the economic infrastructure in place. It's a global effort." I was speaking quickly now. "That's what this research project is about. That's all it is. My professor even has a grant from the Social Sciences and Humanities Research Council for it. SSHRC, we call it, Shirk. It's research. It's completely legitimate. Just like any other research, really. Like cancer research. Biographical, historical research." I was fingering the place mats nervously and I knew I was starting to drone on.

"Look, Mira. We want peace as much as the next person. But the Palestinians are still Israel's enemies. They would wipe us off the map if they could."

Two years earlier, I had sat at this same table the morning after making my way back to my aunt and uncle's house from the apartment of a twenty-seven-year old kibbutznik, a post-army service guy on whom I had a big crush. We had spent most of the night playing cards with his friends, and I felt cool and special, a part of this little Israeli world, on a kibbutz at the foothills of the Gilboa. But I had neglected to tell my aunt where I was, and as the night wore on, she was understandably worried.

"I'm so sorry for not calling. I didn't realize," I had said the next morning, touched by her concern. "I guess this is what it would have felt like to grow up here as a teenager." I laughed. "To attend the American school." Their kibbutz hosted an eleventh-grade program aimed at North American teens. I had seriously considered attending it, but in the end felt frightened about losing my high school social network—which already felt tenuous and subject to the whims of shifting peers and alliances.

"Actually, I was a really square teenager. I always made curfew!" We both smiled, and I felt the warm glow of their loving embrace, as I helped myself to another piece of my aunt's date roll-ups, baked especially for me.

Israeli culture had long connected my aunt and me. When I was ten, I visited my aunt and uncle for three weeks, with my grandmother. In tenth grade, when I was balancing high school social life angst and desperately missing camp, my aunt mailed cassettes of Israeli music to me in

Vancouver. I played them on a loop, eager to absorb the songs of Shlomo Artzi, Arik Einstein, and Yoni Richter. Those tunes had connected us, forming a straight line from the brown polyester Israeli rock band T-shirt, with the face of Izhar Cohen, the singer of the winning Eurovision song "A-ba-Ni-Bi," that she had given me when I was six.

I wonder how my extended family expected anything different: connect me with Israel and send me Israeli folk rock music and send me to the kibbutz school when I am in fifth grade and invite me to spend weekends on the kibbutz when I'm twenty and be proud that I am attending Hebrew University and pick me up from the airport soon after the 1992 elections with Meretz swag in the backseat and generally get me so connected to the place that I actually care. That I actually want to do something about the injustice that I see.

Now, I advance with the crowd toward the sea, clutching the peace flag, and watch the fabric ripple in the light breeze.

A few blocks later, as we are snaking through a side street, coun-terprotesters shout from their apartment balconies. "*Am Yisrael Chai!*" they yell. "The nation of Israel lives!" Now I'm making another mental association with summer camp, where, during the camp-wide Maccabiah competition, we belted out our respective team chants, the judges scrib-bling assessments of who had the most *ruach*, the most spirit, on their clipboards. Here in these narrow streets, we sing our chants in point and counterpoint, and I puzzle over the irony of the competing lyrics. Peace vs. unity. The song of national unity—"Am Yisrael Chai"—that I sung so often as a kid in Jewish school—has now become a song of division, a way to stake out the ground of tribalism.

We marchers want to see a two-state solution, and an end to the occu-pation. I understand the scope of the tension between those Zionists who want to push the government to make land concessions for peace, and those who believe that, in the Palestinians, there is *no partner*. I feel at home in this political debate. But things won't always be so clear to me. One day, I will begin to wonder whether the two-state solution really is the only solution after all. Or whether a more radically just solution— perhaps one that even allows for refugee return and a robust bicultural state—might be called for.

The march winds down: there are speeches and bright lights and a huge plaza. Suddenly I spot someone I recognize. "Gadi!" I shout.

He's been talking to a young girl, his daughter, I presume, and he looks up at me. I look at him expectantly, challenging him to recognize me. We have not seen each other since we were in seventh grade in Jewish day school in Vancouver. He had come to Canada for a few years with his family on sabbatical, before returning to Israel. Like me, he has become an academic; I know as much from Facebook.

He gives me a hug. "Great to see you!"

I switch to Hebrew. "Do you come here often?" I say, and we laugh. I explain that I'm here on a family vacation and that my family has just left. "I mean, do you come to marches often?"

"We try to bring the kids. We try to come as often as we can." He points to his wife, sitting several feet away, and I wave.

"It's getting pretty depressing. The situation," I say.

"Yeah, I mean, man. Ariel College has just gotten university status for fuck's sake. It's insane." Gadi is referring to the post-secondary institution deep in the West Bank. Many Israeli professors had protested the upgrade in status from community college to full-fledged university. Those critics believe that by legitimizing the school even further, Israel's hold over the town that juts deep into the West Bank would be strengthened. Ariel had become an important symbol for those who oppose the occupation. I had followed the issue closely that summer in the news.

"I know what you mean." I shake my head slowly, back and forth.

"Wow. It *is* great to see you," he says.

We promise to keep in touch on Facebook.

I step away, back into the crowd, and turn toward the podium where the first speaker is beginning her address. Signs and placards dominate the sight lines.

Though I am comfortable in the range of the debate tonight, and in musing with an old friend about Ariel College and the occupation, signs and posters about the Israeli-Palestinian conflict sometimes caused me personal grief.

"Those posters are really unfair," I said to Hassan, in the late nineties. He was a fellow Ph.D. student in my department in Washington, DC. He was Arab-American and funny and outgoing. We had an easy friendship. We almost never talked about politics directly—a bit ironic, perhaps, in a graduate program devoted to the study of it—but I knew that we didn't disagree on much. We both opposed the occupation and the Israeli settlements in the West Bank; we both wanted dignity and freedom for Palestinians. Our conversations weren't usually about Israel–Palestine anyway; they were more often about jargony political science stuff: civil society, democratization, and hegemonic transitions. But on this particular afternoon, the topic we'd managed to avoid in any direct sense had seeped out of its drum. And I was arguing for a side I didn't think I'd be on.

That week, posters protesting "fifty years of occupation" had peppered the campus. It was 1998. "Those posters are offensive," I said. "The occupation started in 1967, after the Six-Day War, not in 1948. So we all know what those posters mean by *fifty years of occupation*. They mean that, even within its 1948 borders, the State of Israel has *no right to exist*."

"Forget about this right-to-exist business. It's a red herring," Hassan said. "The occupation started in 1948, and even before. The Israeli state," he said, using the term more common to critics of Israel than the more mainstream term State of Israel, "was founded on the backs of Palestinians."

"But creating an independent, sovereign state is not the same as occupation," I said. "If we call everything occupation then we undermine the meaning of the word. We have to focus on ending the occupation — of the West Bank and Gaza — the real, *actual* military occupation — now. If we want to get anything done, we have to all be in this together. And those signs aren't helping."

We stared at one another, the air thick with tension.

"Look," I continued. "I'm the first to acknowledge that the occupation has to end. But let's get the facts straight. The West Bank and Gaza are occupied. Israel within the Green Line — Israel proper — is not. Israel — Green Line Israel — is a democracy. It's not perfect, but Palestinian citizens of Israel are not under occupation. They are democratic citizens. There's no way you can say that Palestinian citizens of Israel are under occupation. I mean you can say it if you want, but you'd be lying."

"*Democracy*," Hassan said dismissively. "Next you're going to tell me that Israel is the only democracy in the Middle East." Here he lifted his fingers into air quotes. "What year did the Nakba happen?" he asked, without waiting for my answer. "1948. Even before that. You've read Benny Morris," he added, referring to the Israeli historian whose careful research was the first to make Israelis and other non-Palestinians aware of the causes and dynamics of the Palestinian refugee experience. "And Palestine has been occupied by the Zionists ever since."

"Wait. I asked you already but I'll ask you again. Are you saying that Israel — even within the Green Line — has *no right to exist*?"

"That phrase is propaganda," he said. No state has a *right to exist*."

I took a step backward and slid my hand across the smooth paint of the office wall. "How can we ever achieve peace if we don't recognize the national rights and aspirations of *both* peoples? That means that Palestinian refugees can return to a Palestinian state, in the West Bank. If they want to. And Israel can keep its core identity as a Jewish state."

"A *Jewish* state?" he said, his voice rising. "How can a state be both Jewish *and* a democracy? That's an oxymoron!"

I exhaled slowly. "A Jewish state just means a state for the Jewish nation, like any other nation has. Or tries to have. Quebec might want to become a state. Maybe it will one day. The Kurds might one day get their state. If that day comes, will you say that a Quebecois state — or a Kurdish state — is an oxymoron?"

"Look," he said. If you ignore the Nakba, peace will never be achieved. It all started with the Zionist conquest. Expulsion. Dispossession. Murder. Palestinians didn't just walk out of their homes, saying welcome Zionists, enjoy yourselves. There's coffee with cardamom on the counter. And help yourselves to the olives on the tree outside!"

"You're darn right it started earlier," I retorted. "It all started with the pogroms! Never mind the Holocaust." Now I was nearly shouting.

Hassan scowled. "We're talking about the Nakba, not the Holocaust. Let's keep everyone's suffering distinct, here. And let's not mix and match perpetrators. The Palestinians weren't responsible for the Holocaust. Or for the pogroms."

"I know. *Of course* I know that European crimes shouldn't be blamed on the Palestinians. I'm just saying that Jews deserve a state just like Palestinians do." I drew in a sharp breath. "We need to work for a two-state solution. And that means supporting *both* Zionist aspirations and Palestinian national aspirations. Can't we do both? Those posters do not help at all."

I was flustered. I didn't normally even believe in the idea that the State of Israel resulted principally from the Holocaust. Zionist immigration to Palestine had started in the 1880s, with successive waves of aliya. And while antisemitism—culminating in the Holocaust—was an important force, in my dissertation I stressed that the "pull factors" were equally if not more important: the view that modern Zionism resulted from the desire for the Jewish collective to self-actualize, to get their hands dirty and their bodies bronzed working the fields, while literally refashioning the body politic. Jewish nationalism, in other words, was a reflection of so many other nationalisms arising in Europe at that time. It was no better and no worse.

As for the Palestinians, I suppose I had adopted the view that, to the early Zionists, they were mostly invisible.

In graduate school, the most common disputes I engaged in with my classmates were over theoretical models of international relations: whether states behaved according to power and interests alone, or whether those interests were shaped by identities and relationships. In other words, we debated explanatory theories that often seemed disconnected from actual politics. We rarely took a stand on questions of who should do what on the global stage.

And when I did venture into real-world political struggles during my earlier university years, they were usually *within* the Jewish community, where I was used to being the justice-seeker, the peace seeker. At McGill, in undergrad, when I was majoring in Middle East Studies, I had pushed a progressive Zionist line against the more conservative Jewish establishment. I verbally sparred with the students who were active in those Israel advocacy networks. I wrote articles in our little progressive Zionist newsletter. I considered myself fair-minded and analytical, a progressive, a leftist. A progressive, leftist Zionist. So it surprised me, that day of my argument with Hassan, to hear more centrist and even right-leaning arguments coming out of my mouth.

"God, you really don't get it," Hassan said. "Call me when you do. *Fax* me when you really begin to understand the extent of the Nakba." And then Hassan walked away, leaving me standing alone next to the computer nook where, through the glass, I could hear the click-click of keyboards as our fellow grad students checked their email.

I glanced toward my professor's door, which was ajar. My cheeks reddened as I realized he had no doubt heard every word. He specialized in a different region of the world—one with its share of knife-edge tensions. But I had never heard anyone in the halls of my graduate program argue heatedly about the Korean Peninsula.

I began to fear that my relationship with Hassan would never be the same. And part of me must have realized that in this debate about 1948 versus 1967 I had, perhaps for the first time, encountered the limits of Zionism. But I was not yet ready to admit that to myself.

Most of the Israel–Palestine signs these days around my campus in Canada—alongside sexual assault awareness posters and ads for *The Office* trivia pub nights—have abandoned the word "peace" and instead embraced the word "apartheid." In 2009, in the lead-up to Israeli Apartheid Week, an annual Palestine solidarity event held on university campuses around the world, I found myself on the phone with one of the vice presidents at my university. He'd reached out to me, as one of the few Israel–Palestine specialists on campus, for advice.

"There have been complaints about the Israel apartheid week posters," he explained to me. "What are your thoughts?"

I knew the posters he was talking about. The cartoonist had drawn an IDF helicopter aiming a missile directly at a young child wearing a kaffiyeh and clutching a teddy bear.

War between Israel and Hamas had recently ended in a ceasefire, but not before roughly fifteen hundred Palestinians and thirteen Israelis were killed. Israelis had called the war Operation Cast Lead. Many Palestinians simply called it The Gaza Massacre.

"Hmm," I began. "I guess I'd say this. It's understandable that Carleton students want to raise awareness about the war in Gaza. It's terrible what has happened there. It's a massive, tragic loss of life. But because the cartoonist drew the missile as curving from the IDF helicopter *directly at* the Palestinian child, the poster makes it look like Israel is *deliberately targeting* civilians. So while I understand the anger and activism around the violence, I think the image is unfair."

"Some are calling for us to take the posters down," he said.

"That's a tough one. I understand the impulse. But on the other hand, we don't want to get into the business of curtailing free expression among our students when it comes to politics and activism."

"Right. That's the challenge," he said.

I paused as I paced outside my son's bedroom, watching him run a blue car made from recycled plastic across the Ikea rug.

And then I added, "Palestine solidarity activists have every right to express their anger at the IDF. Israel is keeping the West Bank population under occupation. And Gaza is really suffering. But Israel did remove its ground troops and settlers from Gaza in 2005. And Hamas isn't totally blameless here, aiming missiles indiscriminately into Israel. So I guess I'd want us, if we could, to encourage Carleton students to look at the big picture. How can we help everyone — Israelis and Palestinians — live safely?"

"I appreciate your insights," the vice president said.

A few days later, figuring that the image might give rise to violations of the rights enshrined in the Ontario Human Rights Code, the university administration demanded the removal of the posters. Hearing about the announcement, I felt ambivalent. On the one hand, I understood the anger over the carnage in Gaza. On the other, I was annoyed by the crude attempt to cast Israel as murderer of children without any context, without any acknowledgment of Israel's attempt—however limited in practice in a densely-populated area like Gaza—to distinguish between combatants and civilians. And though I probably didn't want to admit it, I felt a pang of protectiveness over the Jewish State on my campus here in Ottawa, my home country but a city that was still new to me, that didn't quite feel like home.

After the speeches have ended, I hand my flag to an organizer and walk the several blocks back to Omri's. He's watching TV news in the living room. I'm buzzed by the evening's events and ready to share my analysis with him and get his take. Omri tells me they didn't end up making the march because Lilach, their young daughter, missed her nap and was exhausted.

"Oh, I hear you. I know what those nap-less days are like. Yeah, it would have been fun to march together. But do you think it was unethical for me to have marched?"

"What do you mean?"

"Well, I'm not actually Israeli, and these peace marches are designed to give citizens an opportunity to signal to the government what they want, right?"

"Well, I guess non-citizens marching does skew the data a little, hypothetically at least."

"But I *do* have a sort of quasi-citizenship, don't I? I mean, Diaspora Jewry and all that. At least Bibi would like the world to think that the Diaspora is part and parcel of Israel. Sometimes, anyway, at least."

I'm thinking about the idea behind the Birthright program, for instance, through which thousands of young Diaspora Jews get a free trip to Israel. Birthright began as an initiative funded by two Jewish philanthropists—including a prominent Canadian Jew, Charles Bronfman—and soon became a joint effort with Israel's own government agencies. Prime Minister Netanyahu frequently gives speeches suggesting that the State of Israel represents world Jewry and is often uncomfortably direct in asserting his role as spokesperson. Addressing Congress just a few weeks earlier, he thanked American lawmakers for their "unwavering support for Israel," claiming, "I speak on behalf of the Jewish people and the Jewish state when I say to you, representatives of America, thank you."

Omri looks away from the TV. "Yeah, Bibi has his own agenda. I wouldn't necessarily follow his lead. More to the point, transnational identity counts for something. But I don't think it totally counts in this case. You don't have a vote here, after all."

I look out the window at the giant palm tree that spans the entire width of the balcony, lit from behind by the streetlights.

"We could write something together," I propose. "About Jewish and Israeli identity. Transnational connection. Thinking about transnational identity as a new citizenship category."

With this invitation, I'm searching for friendly connection, intellectual and social exchange, and a way to matter in my discipline. My first book came out a decade ago, and after raising two young kids, I've been struggling to land on a new research direction and find a new sense of intellectual community.

"I'm not sure I have much to say on this," he says, "but I'd be happy to read something that *you* write." He grins.

Omri and I met several years ago at a conference. He told me he'd read and enjoyed my book, in which I traced Israel's path to making peace with the PLO at Oslo. I was flattered that my social-psychoanalytic theoretical approach seemed to appeal to this smart, young graduate student fresh out of a PhD, and also that, as an actual Israeli, he liked my case study of Israeli policy. I loved sharing my interest in Israel with Israelis who were equally analytical: ones who would appreciate my academic eye because they, too, were trained to examine their country critically.

That night, in Omri's apartment, I sleep fitfully. I miss Steve and the kids. Waking sometime around two a.m., I discover that what I had thought was Omri and Abigail's guest room—restful and breezy, with a pretty blue and white duvet—is actually their master bedroom. A chill goes through me as I realize that Omri and Abigail have given me *their* room while they crowd into their daughter's bedroom, sleeping on foam mats spread across the floor. I'm mortified by my cluelessness and wish I'd offered to sleep on the living room sofa. I jump onto Facebook to contact my writing partner, our common friend. It's still early evening where he is.

"Take them for dinner," he says. "And buy them a nice bottle of wine."

For the rest of the night, I toss and turn, embarrassed by their generosity.

A few days later, I catch a ride to Jerusalem with another friend, who went to McGill with me, and who ended up making her life in Israel, where she works as a pollster and political analyst. She represents one of my few personal roads not taken. This friend has a stylish apartment, also in downtown Tel Aviv, cycles to the beach to swim on Friday afternoons, and is a frequent media analyst. She drops me at the traffic circle in Mevaseret, a suburb just outside Jerusalem. She's on her way to a speaking engagement and I'm meeting Oded Löwenheim, another Israeli friend-colleague. He's writing a book, called *The Politics of the Trail*, about his daily mountain-bike commute to Mount Scopus, using the route as a metaphor for all sorts of political observations.

Oded didn't always cycle to campus. As a student, he took the bus. But one morning, in August 1995, he was running to catch the bus as he saw it pull away. He gave chase for half a block before giving up. Twenty-five minutes later, at 7:45 a.m., as he'd learn while hearing the radio broadcast on the bus he did end up catching, the bus he was supposed to be on exploded. A female suicide bomber had detonated her vest on board as the vehicle was snaking through the Ramat Eshkol neighborhood. The bomb killed four passengers and wounded a hundred others. Traumatized by his near-miss, Oded pledged never to ride the bus again. Since his wife uses the car to shuttle their kids to and from school, he decided to become a cycling commuter, riding his mountain bike along the dusty Jerusalem hills from his home to his office. It's a tale he's recounted in a 2010 article he published in the *International Studies Review*.

"Hey," Oded greets me through the window. I introduce him to my other friend; she's anxious to get on her way. I jump into the passenger seat of Oded's car and give him a quick hug.

"*Tov lir'ot otcha*," I say. It's good to see you. I'm looking forward to spending an afternoon speaking Hebrew.

"So? You ready for a day of touring?" Oded asks. I nod eagerly.

He'd promised to take me on his regular tour. I was excited about the idea of doing it by bike, like he does, but the logistics of outfitting me with the right gear seemed daunting, so we've planned to do the tour by car and on foot.

Starting in the Halilim wadi, the valley of the flutes, we perch on the edge of a stone terrace as Oded tells me the legend of the flute. "The daughter of the village mukhtar longs to marry a poor shepherd, despite her father's protestations. So the girl's father sets out a challenge for the boy: if he succeeds in herding the father's flock, they will be permitted to marry."

I think about the kind of fairy tales I grew up with, which were sometimes feminist versions of classic stories—like on the *Free to Be You and Me* record I listened to at my parents' house, and then, after their divorce, at my mom's house. At my dad's house, there were different records: Simon and Garfunkel, The Beatles.

Oded is telling me an old-fashioned tale, and I try not to settle into assumptions about the Palestinians being overly traditional, being Other. I've read enough Edward Said to know the dangers of Orientalism, of Othering. But I can't escape the sense that I'd rather be drinking wine with Oded on a sidewalk cafe in Tel Aviv, away from the tension of traditional tales and political jostling over rocks and dirt.

"Next, we'll go to Lifta," Oded says, pulling me out of my reverie. I shake myself back to the present and realize that I am, after all, grateful to explore these places with a guide who is as sensitive and patient and excited about the hidden politics of Jerusalem as Oded is. Lifta refers to the remains of a Palestinian village near the western entrance to Jerusalem. It's now a collection of stone buildings nestled into a ridge. Israelis are familiar with it—schoolchildren in the area go there for nature field trips, and it's been in the news recently. Jewish squatters have moved in, and now developers are eyeing it as a spot for upscale residences. But the historical circumstances of the village are less often talked about. Like hundreds of other villages and towns around what is now Israel, Lifta was once populated by Palestinians. The 1948 war for Israeli independence involved massive expulsion and fleeing of Palestinians at the hands of Israeli forces—roughly 750,000 Palestinians would become refugees by the war's end. Palestinians would come to call this period the Nakba. Israelis would refer to it as simply 1948, or *milchemet hashichrur*, the war of liberation.

When we arrive, we park and walk down a steep path toward the village. At the entrance to the area, Hebrew graffiti greets us: "Kahane was right," it says, referring to Meir Kahane, the far-right, racist politician who immigrated to Israel from the United States and had been banned from the Knesset for his fundamentalist policies before being assassinated in New York City by an Arab-American who later confessed to the crime.

Oded and I glance away from the graffiti and toward each other, with eyebrows raised. Recent graffiti around Jerusalem and Tel Aviv has become chatty and political, with stenciled images of Theodore Herzl's profile and missives about who was actually right: Kahane or Yeshayahu Leibowitz. Leibowitz was the dovish political philosopher who urged Israelis to reckon with the fate of the Palestinian territories captured in the Six-Day War. It's heady stuff for graffiti. But nothing is dull in Israel.

Soon we spot two young men wearing acid-wash jeans and polo-style shirts. "Hi," we say, eyeing them. Their body language and dress suggests they are Palestinian. Our curiosity is aroused.

"Are you from here? Nearby?" Oded asks, in Hebrew.

"My family is from Lifta," one of the men says with an Arabic accent.

I do some quick calculations in my head. It's 2011. If he's around twenty-five now, then he would have been born in the late eighties, during the first Intifada. His parents most likely would have born in the late fifties or early sixties, which means the last adults in his family to have lived in Lifta would have been his great-grandparents. Given that he's still here in Jerusalem, his grandparents, as children, along with their parents, likely ended up a mile over in East Jerusalem, which was under Jordanian rule until 1967, when Israel conquered it.

Oded probes further. "How do you feel about being here, visiting your old town?"

His answer surprises us. "*Mah sheh haya, haya*," he says. What's done is done.

We nod uncertainly, trying to signal that we understand these two young men we've just met more deeply than perhaps they assume we, as Jewish Israelis, would normally understand them. I have remained mostly quiet. My accent would give me away as not being Israeli. But we don't really buy what they're saying.

"I guess," Oded says.

We look at each other for another moment. The past has a powerful way of carrying memory and burying it, I think to myself.

I suddenly feel moved to get one last question in. "So you're just visiting, hanging out here?"

They nod. "Yeah, just hanging."

We pause again, hoping for more. But the moment seems to have passed.

"So take care, all the best," Oded says.

"Yallah, bye," we say in unison, the Arabic-English-Hebrew hybrid sign-off common in Israel.

I look over at Oded. Most Israelis wouldn't bother engaging with strangers who appear to be Palestinians, never mind asking them how they feel about the layered history of this land. But Oded is different. He's thoughtful, smart, and uncertain, filled with more questions than answers. It's an unusual combination, especially for an Israeli man, at least in my experience of living here for a few years in my twenties. I will soon learn that the typical markers of Israeli masculinity—the bravado, the military pedigree—indeed differ in Oded's case, in surprising ways.

"That was weird," he says to me. "Were they trying to appease us, do you think?"

"I don't know. They seemed like they didn't want us to probe further. Who knows what they were really thinking? And of course, there's a power difference we shouldn't forget about."

"Of course," he says. "They don't know who we are. We could be undercover officers. Maybe they snuck in through a hole in the fence and were worried about being caught."

A minute later, we arrive at the village spring. Several Orthodox Jewish men have gathered. Some are beginning to undress. I briefly consider my options. I could stay and stake my ground. I could stay and turn away. Or I could leave. I decide to retreat. But not before entertaining a streak of resentment that their religious practices seem to infringe on my right, as a woman, to be here.

Oded and I walk back up the hill toward the city, where his car is parked.

We spend the rest of the afternoon talking about Israeli Jews, about Palestinians, about what it's like to live in a country with layers of privilege, increasing religious fundamentalism, and the lurking threat of violence. We talk about our respective identities. I tell him about the peace march last night in Tel Aviv and how I felt betwixt and between. I long to be part of this community even as I relish my outsider status. I am proud of my Hebrew—and grateful for my native English. And I love to explore these complexities with Oded, a fellow academic who is just as interested in the nuances as I am.

I adore the insider-outsider feeling I have in Israel. Here, at least among Jews, no one really feels like a stranger. There was the store-keeper at the *makolet*, the corner store in Tel Aviv the other night, who asked while ringing up my order of fresh apricots, dried dates, and a pink Gillette shaver—I'd forgotten to pack mine from Ottawa for my trip—about the scar on my arm.

"Melanoma. Skin cancer. When I was twenty-one," I explained in Hebrew. The word for cancer, *sartan,* is the same as the word for crab. It's a connection I learned in our horoscope unit in fourth grade. Cancer—the crab symbol—is my dad's sign. My mom's a scorpio. I'm a gemini.

"Ah, I'm so sorry," the shopkeeper said, looking at me intently as he bagged my items. And then, like a long-lost cousin, he said to me, "You should only be well. May you have good health and a long life."

Oded and I linger on a park bench at one of the picnic spots popular among Israelis on vacation days. We are talking about growing up. He points across the park to a multi-layered cemetery—there simply isn't enough room to bury everyone on one flat surface here in Jerusalem, he explains—where his father was recently buried. We talk about high school, and what it was like for him, growing up in Jerusalem.

"What did you do in the army?" I ask. I am sure it was something prestigious: the Paratroopers, maybe. Intelligence. The Air Force. Maybe the Armored Corps, surely something high status. Maybe he'd even remained after his obligatory three years of duty to become an officer.

He looks down. "Uh, I had a desk job. Menial tasks. Nothing glamorous."

I'm almost sure he is pulling my leg.

"Why are you looking at me that way?" he asks.

"*Stam.*" No reason.

I look away, embarrassed, realizing I've been projecting the same macho, status-seeking expectations I seek to conquer in my ordinary life. The patriarchy. Constructed masculinity. But here, in Israel, I have absorbed them.

I wore those values literally when I was twenty—in the form of a threadbare cotton T-shirt I had found when I first arrived on the kibbutz of my youth movement, where I spent weekends while at Hebrew University. Rifling through a basket of old work clothes, I held up a red shirt to the light. It was soft and worn, with a silkscreened military insignia over the left breast. An IDF paratroopers unit. Induction date: November 1984. Those soldiers would be twenty-six or so now.

The next day, a twenty-something kibbutznik, broad-shouldered, with long, dirty blond hair tied back in a bandana, walked toward me. "Hey, that's my shirt," he said.

"Is that okay with you?" I asked, flashing him a smile.

"Is it okay with *you*?" The corners of his mouth turned upward.

"It's okay with me only if *you* deserve to have *me* wear your shirt." I smoothed my hair.

He didn't protest, so I slipped it into my bag, grinning at him over my shoulder.

I wore that shirt for years—until it was in tatters and beyond. The red cotton was similar to a life jacket I had once worn, but the feeling couldn't have been more different.

When I was four or five, my dad took me to my great-uncle's cottage for the weekend. They had four kids, all older than me. The only life jacket that fit me was the red cotton kind popular in the seventies, the kind that you squeeze over your head and has a big fat piece that sits behind your neck. I hated that life jacket. My cousins all had grown-up sporty kinds, made out of orange nylon, and that zipped up in front. With its fat neck piece and childish strings, that cotton life jacket reminded me of my otherness. I was younger, I was an only child, I didn't know how to drive a motorboat, I didn't have a family cottage, I didn't have a big split-level house in River Heights with modular furniture and built-in lockers with my initials for all my sports equipment. And most of all, I didn't have parents who were still married to each other.

That army shirt I found on the kibbutz wasn't only about feeling cool and tough. It made me feel like I belonged, just like the army-issued pants, stamped *tzahal*, IDF, that had somehow come into my possession when I was in high school. I wore those pants at Hebrew summer camp, half hoping they had been smuggled out of Israel and that I was holding international contraband, and half hoping they were imitation, because I didn't like to think I was breaking any law.

"I despised my time in the army," Oded says, smoothing out a spot of chipped paint on the back of the park bench. "I didn't want to be there. I didn't try for a prestigious combat position. I did grunt work. I swept floors. I couldn't wait to get out of there."

"Wow," I say. "I never knew. I guess I just assumed … " I trail off. His eyes are intense and suddenly I can't hold his gaze without feeling my heart race, ever so slightly.

Soon, Oded and I become even closer. The kind of colleague-friends who share article drafts and guest speak in one another's classes and debrief afterwards, and who reveal personal struggles to one another. He writes me long, detailed emails in Hebrew, and I write long, detailed emails back in English.

In 2015, he sends me a link to an essay he's published in the *Journal of Narrative Politics*. It describes his time in the army with great candor. He had told me a little about those unglamorous years while we were sitting on that park bench, and now it's here, laid out for all to see. I read the essay, eagerly. And then I share it with my network. I'm proud of this Israeli friend of mine who is adventurous enough to mountain bike to work, and who is confident enough to reveal his vulnerabilities publicly. And I am flattered that he shared these stories with me first. It turns out that his sensitivity and intelligence are much more appealing to me than the prototypical elite sabra masculinity that Israeli society so often promotes, and that I had naively believed I was drawn to when I flirted on kibbutz with the tough guys who jockeyed with me for their combat unit shirts.

"Why do we seem to tell each other things that we tell almost no one else?" I ask Oded, at one of our later meetings, when I am back in Israel on another research trip.

"It's just sort of become that way," he says, as he sips a bowl of soup and I nurse a glass of pinot grigio at a Jerusalem restaurant. "It's hard to know these things."

In our friendship, there is none of the ritual dance of showmanship and bravado so common in my casual interactions with Israelis who populate the society I long to be a part of but am not. Oded acts like he has nothing to prove to me, and ends up proving that what I most crave is a friend across the Israeli Diaspora divide. Someone who accepts me, with all my Diaspora awkwardness and my attempts at sounding Israeli when I speak Hebrew and my striving to have a voice and be part of this society that's not quite mine but isn't quite not mine, either. Someone who thinks I matter, in all my wholeness.

CHAPTER 2

Carpets

1976

My eyes dart from my mom to my dad and back again, before landing on the toys, games, books, records, and stuffed animals that are spread out along the green carpet, forming a rough circle. The seams of the lid to Hi-Ho Cherry-O are ripped, and little plastic cherries have spilled out of the box.

My mom speaks first. "Put the toys you want to keep at Mommy's place here," she says, pointing to a spot near the window, "and the toys you want to take to Daddy's place there." She gestures toward the foyer, but her arm drops limply to her side.

My mom's instructions take a few seconds to land. I don't understand what it means to have a daddy's place and a mommy's place. Until now, this house with the green carpet, this house with my brown bedspread with the little lines I like to run my hand over, the house with my Fisher Price record player and my arts and crafts supplies and the dresses that I prefer not to wear—because I prefer my jeans and long-sleeved shirts with iron-on Sesame Street patches, except when I held my mom's hand while we wore matching outfits for a fashion show at the mall because I liked having all eyes on me—has been a home for the three of us.

My dad crouches down and leans toward me. "Mommy and Daddy are getting separated," he says. "But we both still love you very much." His eyes look wet.

© The Author(s) 2021
M. Sucharov, *Borders and Belonging: A Memoir*,
https://doi.org/10.1007/978-3-030-53732-6_2

Getting separated. I hear the words and my brow furrows. I know I'm supposed to separate my clean clothes from my dirty clothes. I know that at McDonald's there are separate bathrooms for girls and boys. Usually I like my mom to separate the yolk from the white part of the egg before I eat it. I know that Jews are supposed to separate milk from meat. But I can't picture my parents *getting separated.* Suddenly the phrase sounds shameful. My cheeks feel hot.

My hand wanders to the scab near my lip where I cut myself the other week because I went into my parents' bathroom and found my dad's razor and tried to shave my chin just like he does. I remember blood dripping as I stared at my reflection in the mirror, climbing up onto the sink to get a better look.

If I refuse to pick out toys for Daddy's place and for Mommy's place, I wonder, will my parents decide not to *get separated*? I look up at my mom and she lowers her gaze. Her jaw is clenched in the way I recognize when she's upset, and soon she wipes away a tear with the back of her hand.

We live in the south end of Winnipeg, on a small, crescent-shaped street called Lanark Bay. If my parents get separated, will I have to move? Maybe somewhere else in the south end? Maybe to the north end, where my dad grew up? I look outside, through the screen door, near the spot where our neighbor's housekeeper had yanked me high up off the ground when she found me playing with the red and orange nasturtiums on their front-porch flower beds made of white brick and oozing mortar. My eyes widened as she shouted at me and I tried my hardest not to cry.

I scan my games. I pick up Trouble, Mousetrap, and Mr. Mouth and carry them to the Daddy's place pile. To the meager collection, he adds a bag of Lego and two stuffed animals and four Little Golden Books and three Mr. Men books. To read to me at bedtime, he says. I can hear his voice crack and I blink back tears.

"Will I sleep at Daddy's place too, sometimes?" I ask. I don't bother to listen to the answer because now I am crying. I hate this *getting separated*.

My mom and dad got married in the gymnasium at the Jewish school in the North End six years before I was born. Their wedding picture hangs in my baba's apartment, next to my uncle and aunt's wedding picture, and above my dad and my uncle's Bar Mitzvah photos. Will Baba take down the wedding photo?

Not long after my dad moves out, I am at Grant Park Plaza with my mom and I'm licking a chocolate-vanilla twist ice-cream cone when I spot a man in a wheelchair out of the corner of my eye. He has gray hair and gray pants and a white shirt and, as I look sideways toward his lap, I see that he has a stump where his right leg should be.

Suddenly, my guts begin to swirl. I look away from the missing leg and then back again once more, just to be sure. Now my insides feel like there are flames burning my tummy and my heart is pounding and I need to escape. I hand my mom my ice-cream cone as I squeeze my eyes shut. "Can we go home now?" I ask.

A few months later, my mom says we have to go to the Bay department store for *errands*. By now it's almost winter, and it's dark and cold and the days end early. As I climb out of my mom's car in the downtown parking garage, my guts begin to swirl again and the flames come back. I am trying not to look toward the entrance of the Bay because there might be people coming out. And where there are lots of people, there might be someone crippled or someone else in a wheelchair or someone missing an arm or an ear or even a finger.

"Don't make me go in there. Please don't make me go in there. I can't go in there!" I am yelling through my tears and my nose is running. I grab onto my mom's neck. When I realize I've lost the battle and we are going in anyway, I try to force myself to sleep on her shoulder. This is the only way I can get through the war.

A few days later, I am at my dad's downtown apartment, not far from the parking garage where I forced myself to sleep on my mom's shoulder. My dad has traded the green carpet in what used to be a house for the three of us for a blue carpet here, in this apartment in this high-rise building with an elevator. This apartment is mostly for my dad, but sometimes it's for me too.

Since his apartment is connected to the Holiday Inn, he and I are allowed to use the hotel swimming pool, where I wear a yellow bathing suit and perform somersaults from the pool edge into the deep end. Then we sit in the jacuzzi to warm up and watch people swimming and lounging, some of whom live in the apartments and some of whom are tourists. After swimming, my dad buys me a pack of Old Dutch ripple chips. As I eat the chips, I remain on the lookout for crippled people or people missing a limb.

Over the sofa in his apartment with the blue carpet my dad has hung a picture of clocks that look like they are melting on a beach, except there is a block of concrete on the sand, and jutting out from that block is a tree with no leaves. One clock hangs over the tree branch, a second hangs over the edge of the block, and a third is draped over a giant piece of driftwood. I mostly keep my back to the picture because I prefer to face the TV. Last week my mom had phoned my dad to tell us to turn on the TV because there was a new show that just came out and it had puppets and music and even Kermit the Frog, who we already knew from *Sesame Street*. This new program was called *The Muppet Show*, my mom said. So we turned on the TV to watch it together, my dad and me at Daddy's place, and my mom at Mommy's place.

Usually I like watching TV at my dad's. But tonight I don't. We're watching a Disney movie and I soon have to turn away from that, and face the melty painting that is a little scary but less scary than the movie. The movie, called *Now You See Him, Now You Don't*, is making my heart beat a thousand times per minute and the flames are licking my guts again. In the film, a man has invented a potion that can make people seem invisible. But when the actor who my dad says is Kurt Russell dips his finger into a glass of the invisibility potion and pulls it out, it looks to me like his finger has been amputated. Now the flames are back and I just want to escape out of my skin and be somewhere else or become someone else. Someone who doesn't have to sit in the back seat of her mom's compact car that her mom calls a *lemon*, that belongs only to her mom and not to her dad too, and then ride in an elevator to visit her dad, who has a pool, but it's not really our pool, not like the little plastic one my dad used to fill with the garden hose and that belonged to all three of us in the backyard of the house with the green carpet along with a red and white metal swing set with a little white seesaw where I could give my stuffed animals a ride if I wanted to, without worrying about which ones were still at Mommy's place and which ones were at Daddy's.

Soon my parents tell me I have a *phobia* of crippled people or people who are missing a limb. They take me to see a psychiatrist named Dr. Weinstein. I'm only a little bit scared about seeing a psychiatrist but not very scared, because my dad is a psychiatrist too.

Dr. Weinstein invites me into her office and points to a small table with a chair, just like I've seen at my Montessori preschool. As I sit down, she hands me a sheet of paper. Then she slides a can filled with crayons toward me. I clutch the crayons and smooth out the paper and draw a three-headed person. "Beautiful artwork, Mira," Dr. Weinstein says, with a smile. "Tell me a bit about it."

I look at my drawing and then into Dr. Weinstein's smooth face. I point to the paper. "This is my family." My voice is quiet.

"Tell me more about your family," she says.

"This is me, this is my mom, and this is my dad," I say, pointing to each figure in turn.

Dr. Weinstein nods and writes some notes on a clipboard.

The next day, my dad holds up my drawing and looks at me. "Dr. Weinstein says that this picture means you feel like our family is a person who has come apart."

I nod, while blinking back tears.

"Maybe this is what explains your phobia of crippled people," my dad says. "They remind you of our family. Do you feel our family came apart when Mommy and Daddy separated?" He is nodding sympathetically.

I begin to cry, and my dad hugs me.

Not long after, my mom and I say goodbye to the green-carpet house and we move into a duplex. It is still in the south end, but in a different neighborhood. We live on a street called Kingsway. I like the name. It reminds me of a castle. My best friend Melanie lives two streets over, on Dromore. That street reminds me of a camel.

Sometimes I ride my bike over to Melanie's house. One afternoon, her mom invites me to stay for dinner. She has made shepherd's pie, and Melanie and I laugh about the name of that dish for no reason at all for five straight minutes and we can't even eat we are laughing so hard. Shepherd's pie. Shepherd's pie. Melanie's mom is annoyed that we are laughing instead of eating. She is already annoyed that we use the word "like" all the time when we talk. She tries to get us to say three sentences without using the word. "Do you mmmmmm the shepherd's pie?" I say to Melanie, keeping my mouth tightly shut where the word "like" should be. And we laugh even harder.

Melanie's mom has *connections*. One afternoon, my mom takes me to Melanie's house, into Melanie's bedroom, where women directors and men with giant cameras are waiting. Melanie's mom works for CBC, so Melanie and I are going to be on an episode of *Sesame Street*. One of the directors wets my hair. Then she hands me a comb and a blow dryer and instructs me to stand in front of the mirror on top of Melanie's dresser. I start drying my hair while combing it out, like I've seen hairdressers do. But I'm not very experienced at combing while blow-drying, and I fumble the comb and it drops to the floor. I bend down to pick it up. "Oops, I dropped the comb," I say. "Can we start again?"

But the directors like the version they've caught on camera. It's *realistic*, they say. You're a kid.

I don't want to be a realistic little kid. I want to be a mature, capable, grown-up kid.

For years afterwards, I watch that clip, which they inserted into some Canadian versions of the show—with Melanie shampooing her hair in the bathtub and me blow-drying my hair in her room and dropping my comb, and clips of other kids playing on the monkey bars with their hair blowing in the wind and a soundtrack behind us with a chorus singing a song about hair and all the things you can do with it, and I like being a bit famous but I don't like being young and realistic, until one day I appreciate the charm of it all, and I understand what the directors were going for.

Our house on Kingsway has hardwood floors instead of carpets, and a screened-in porch where I like to clean my bike with a rag like I've seen Fonzie do with his motorcycle on *Happy Days*. Sometimes I call myself Spike, after Fonzie's nephew. When the neighbors tell my mom that they met her daughter Spike, my mom is confused.

On Saturday nights, my mom gets a babysitter for me so she can go out on dates. So she can have a *social life*, she says.

To prepare for the babysitter, who is a teenage boy with brown eyes and brown skin and who comes every Saturday night, I take down my blue Childcraft encyclopedia from my bedroom shelf. Volume 11. *Make and Do.* I pick out a project for us. There are instructions on how to make a little boat from a walnut shell, a necklace from spools of thread, and a parade of soldiers from toilet-paper rolls. There are designs for building a secret hideaway, a Medieval castle, a submarine, and an entire cardboard house just like the one on the Brady Bunch. There are chalk pictures, finger-painted ones, soapsuds paintings, and artwork using dough. There are recipes for making clay animals, for carving a turtle out of a bar of soap, for fashioning lanterns out of construction paper and for building stick puppets.

This babysitter is a lot nicer than the babysitter we once had in the house with the green carpet. One night at that house, when I said I didn't have to go pee before bed, he locked me in the bathroom and made me sit on the toilet while I cried. When my mom and Dad got home, I told them what he had done and they got mad at him and he never babysat for me again.

Soon my mom buys another house. This one has brown carpet and two peony bushes in the front yard and a tiny fish fossil imprint on the stone fireplace. It's still in the south end but in a different neighborhood, halfway between the other two houses we lived in. This street is called Niagara and it makes me think of Niagara Falls. In this house my mom gets me a new babysitter. But one night she tells me that I wasn't polite because she heard me telling the babysitter, who isn't Jewish, that Jews are luckier than Christians because on Chanukah we get eight days of presents, while on Christmas, Christians only get one.

On the insides of my bedroom drawers at this new house I paste stickers of Han Solo and Luke Skywalker that come in wax-paper packages, along with a thin stick of bubble gum, in the Star Wars cards I collect each Saturday when I get my allowance. I prefer grape Bubble Yum or Strawberry Hubba Bubba to the Star Wars gum. The other gums are chewier and keep their flavor longer. But I love *Star Wars*, the movie, most of all. For Purim last year, my dad helped me make a C-3PO costume from shoeboxes encased in gold wrapping paper.

In these drawers, I no longer have my Sesame-Street-iron-on-patch shirts. Now I have lots of favorite T-shirts. One has a comic strip on it, another has M-I-R-A ironed onto the front, and another is brown and white with the face of an Israeli rock star plastered across it. My aunt sent me that one from Israel. She told my mom to tell me that the singer won a prize for singing a song in Hebrew pig latin. *Abanibi* it's called. I know English pig latin and I now wonder what Hebrew pig latin sounds like.

That June, my dad comes over to my mom's to help run my birthday party. My birthday is on June 8th, and until this year, I thought my birthday had a special name: June-lee-eight. My dad hands me a package. I rip open the paper and inside is a soccer ball. I run my fingers over the black and white pentagons and hexagons as I inhale the smell of the new leather. I can't wait to kick the ball with my dad when we're next at the park.

For my party, my dad has rented reel-to-reel Disney movies to screen for my friends and me in the basement so it can feel like a real movie theater. I've picked the movie *The Rescuers* because it doesn't have any disappearing body parts that look like amputations. I still have my fears.

Soon my parents send me to a different psychiatrist. This one is a friendly man named Dr. James, who has an accent that my dad explains is Australian. His office is next to my dad's. My dad keeps Fisher Price toys in his own office for his youngest patients, who I never get to meet because it's private. My dad tells me about play therapy. I don't know how he can play during the workday when he wears corduroy blazers and wool ties, but I guess he has a way. Dr. James prefers board games.

As I climb the stairs to Dr. James's office, I glance toward my dad's office, but it's evening and he's not there anymore. I sit down on the black leather sofa in Dr. James's office and face him.

Dr. James cocks his head to one side and says, "What's bugging you?" His face is warm but his question makes my guts swirl a little. I shrug. My heart is starting to race.

Everything is bugging me. I hate that my dad no longer lives with my mom. I hate that before each appointment with Dr. James, my mom takes me for dinner to the Charter House restaurant downtown, near my dad's apartment building, but all I can do is stare at my food. At the restaurant, pinballs ricochet off the inside walls of my chest. I dread this appointment.

After a few seconds of silence, Dr. James smiles and turns toward the office shelves. "Shall we play a round of Life?" He pulls down a flat box.

I shrug again. The goals of that game—marriages and mortgages—don't interest me much. But I offer a smile as I get off the couch and sit cross-legged on the brown carpet. I hate having to go to a psychiatrist but I still want Dr. James to like me. I face him across the board and arrange my tiny plastic car with tiny plastic people on the track and take my turn on the spinner that's like the giant one they have on *The Price Is Right* and the time passes easily enough until Dr. James tells me that our session is up and he'll see me next week.

I am the only kid in my grade at school whose parents are divorced. I might be the only one who sees a psychiatrist, too, except I recently heard at recess that Lara does, but it was whispered from Leah to Jenny and then to me. And then I heard Lara herself talking about it in a loud voice that made me suspicious; it almost sounded like she was bragging, and I don't want to be associated with her problems anyway.

Usually I like standing out. But not for this reason.

Soon enough, winter gives way to spring and now it's June and it's warm and sunny and I am on a field trip at a park with my class and we are running and running across a field and suddenly I feel a pair of arms scoop me up and the person is continuing to run with me in the same direction. I hear my dad's voice and feel his strong arms and I'm so excited because this means that summer vacation is here and we are going to his friend's cottage where there are other kids my age and we can jump from the roof of their shed onto piles of leaves and it feels like a family. It's more fun there than at my mom's house where Dimitri, her boyfriend with a beard, sometimes stays over. My mom isn't very happy when Dimitri is around. Sometimes he yells loudly and she yells back. Summer means more time to play with my dad's family friends.

We are running and running and my blood is pumping in the happy way and it's exactly the opposite from what used to happen last year but sort of similar. When I had *whooping cough*, I would faint. And pee my pants. And projectile vomit. And once, I was so weak I fainted in the snow, downtown, and my mom had to try to pick me up and carry me to the doctor's and a man on the street had to help her. And my baba would send me tapes from Vancouver, like letters, except that they were her voice, and she would try to cheer me up about my whooping cough by telling me stories of the whooping cough she had as a little girl in Winnipeg. There, she would help her father deliver cattle to the local farmers. "Whoop, Whoop, Whoop!" she would say as she described the sound of her cough as she rode on his wagon. "The wonderful air, the nice sweet smell of the spring, the grass and the flowers, sure helped my whoop-whoop-whooping cough!"

But at the beginning of the summer, my mom comes into my room with a worried look. "Pack some clothes and some books," she says. "We're going to Vancouver. To stay with Baba and Zaida."

"How long are we going for?"

"Maybe a few weeks. Maybe longer." She is vague.

After the flight where I am allowed a cup of ginger ale to ward off airsickness, we walk up the sidewalk to my grandparents' Vancouver bungalow. "Thank goodness you got away from that man," my baba says to my mom, as she hugs me. As she says "man," I hear "Russian," and then feel guilty for thinking thoughts that are prejudiced.

I know she is talking about Dimitri, who, my mom has explained to me before, is a Russian Jew. I figure that being a Russian Jew is different from being a Canadian or American Jew, and different still from being an Israeli Jew, because here we speak English and there, in Israel, they speak Hebrew like my Hebrew teachers do.

My mom, who has been going to university to learn how to be an interior designer, finds a job in Vancouver organizing the furniture installation at a downtown building project. At my baba and zaida's house, my mom sleeps in her old bedroom—the one with a purple bedspread at the end of the hall. I stay in my aunt's old bedroom, the middle one, with a red and orange striped bedspread. The bed has sliding doors in the headboard where I can stick my fingers in the round metal handles and slide the little doors back and forth. The bedspread has a musty smell that tickles my nose. I lie on the bed and look around. I spot a typing book on the bookshelf and flip through it. I find my baba's old typewriter and bang out a few lines of FFF, JJJ, FJFJ, FFJJ, and promise myself I'll continue onto Lesson Two tomorrow.

The next day, I find a learn-to-speak Spanish book and I work on learning some of the vocabulary. I make flashcards and practice my times tables. I take a jacuzzi in my grandparents' ensuite. In the mornings, I go to drama classes for kids at the nearby high school, and in the afternoons I play tennis with my baba at the neighborhood courts, but I can never win a point.

One afternoon, I am sitting with my baba and zaida on their back patio lined with green miniature-golf carpeting. The air smells like freshly mown grass and jasmine, and I am drinking a mug of hot chocolate, and eating a bowl of my baba's homemade applesauce with bits of peel still in it, and munching on a slice of whole wheat toast spread with cream cheese, which my baba has cut into quarters. My zaida is reading the newspaper. Suddenly, from beyond the laurel hedges, a wasp comes into view, and I swat at it. I feel a sharp pain on my forearm. "Ow!" I shriek. My baba takes me in her arms as I let my tears flow for the wasp sting and for having to escape our house for the summer and for the *separating*.

When my mom and I return home to Winnipeg at the end of the summer, we park in the back lane of our Niagara Street house and enter through the side. My mom fiddles with the key and then the screen door presses against my back and suddenly I hear my mom gasp. I look down. There is a trail of reddish-brown spots along the gray painted wood stairs leading to the basement. The spots look like paint but I know they aren't.

"What are those spots, Mom?" I ask quietly.

"It's probably Dimitri, the *bastard*. Go to your room. You shouldn't see this."

Bastard. It is the only time I have ever heard my mom use that word.

Dimitri had punched through the window while we were away. The drops were blood from his forearm as he came up and down the stairs in search of us. I look down at the spot on my arm where the wasp stung me a couple of weeks earlier.

I go to my room and close the door, lie on my bedspread, and flip on my Little Professor calculator game. Seven x four appears on the numbered display. I type in twenty-eight, enjoying the feeling of the little rectangular plastic buttons under my fingertips. Then I scan my shelves, looking for a new book to read. I settle on *Otherwise Known as Sheila the Great* and get through six pages before my eyes begin to close. I crawl under the covers, turn off my lamp, and wait for my mom to come and tuck me in. I try as hard as I can to forget about the *Bastard* so I won't have bad dreams.

A few months later, a tall man with a mustache starts coming by the house. "Mirtz, this is Ron," my mom says. My mom laughs a lot when Ron is around. Ron starts sleeping over on our living room sofa, helping to protect us. Ron can't pronounce the nickname my mom uses for me, so he calls me Mertz.

Ron and my mom play lots of Scrabble. Ron takes me to the driving range to practice real golf swings, and to amusement centers to play miniature golf where we keep score on little cards. We eat mint-chocolate-chip ice cream, and pepperoni and pineapple pizza. On road trips to Ron's sales conferences to Brandon, Manitoba, the three of us play word games, me in the back seat of his green Buick, and he and my mom in the front. At those sales conferences, Ron sends me to visit the other booths, armed with sunglasses and lip balm, samples that I am allowed to trade for boxes of Turtles and After Eights. Ron gets excited when I bring back the candy. He has a *sweet tooth*, my mom tells me.

Ron and my mom get married the next summer at the Winnipeg conservatory in the park, where I am a flower girl and wear a custom dress in beige cotton eyelet with spaghetti straps and my hair is cut into a silky bob. I pose for photos where the air is humid with sprinklers and greenery. Now I have one mom, one dad, and one stepdad, and I'm relieved that my home feels safer because my stepdad has made my mom and me feel less frightened and we've put bars on the basement windows so the *Bastard* can't hurt us. But I still have some fears.

One Saturday morning, my mom looks at me across my bowl of Cheerios. Ron is sitting next to her, eating oatmeal. She is eating her favorite breakfast: a soft-boiled egg broken into a bowl, mixed with small squares of ripped up toast. Later that day I'll head to the YMHA for an afternoon of activities with my friends, as I do every Saturday.

"I have something important to tell you," my mom says. I look up at her. I bite the inside of my cheek. She goes on to explain that somewhere out there, I have a brother. A half brother. "I had a baby a year before you were born. Daddy and I gave it up for adoption."

"Is it Daddy's baby too?" I ask. I'm not sure what it means to have a half brother, exactly.

"No," she says. "The father is a man I met in Montreal. He worked at a bank. Daddy and I were having problems in our marriage. We were all so young."

I nudge the remaining Cheerios against the side of my bowl. I look over at Ron and he shoots me a sympathetic look. I am no longer hungry. I glance at my silver digital watch. I have to get to the YMHA soon because the club meetings are about to start, and then there's gym and swim, and then pottery and magic and silk screening. I wonder if I'll feel brave enough to tell Leah about this news when I see her later today. I am partly excited to hear this news about a brother. I've always wanted a brother or a sister. Most of the families I read about in my chapter books—books by Beverly Cleary, Judy Blume and John D. Fitzgerald—are about families with more than one kid. Even Fudge, the annoying younger brother in *Tales of a Fourth Grade Nothing*, sounds like he'd be a bit fun to be around. But one of my favorite books is *Are You There God, It's Me, Margaret*, and Margaret is an only child. And so is the character in *Confessions of an Only Child* by Norma Klein. And so is the daughter in *Mom, the Wolf Man, and Me*. But maybe this news means I'm no longer an only child after all. And do Ron's kids count too, as siblings? I'm not really sure.

I had always thought that my mom and dad got separated because they were stressed out about being married so young and about my dad being unhappy in medical school and my mom working a lot. But maybe the separation had something to do with this baby. It's all a little too much for me to figure out so I push it out of my mind.

Eventually, the bastard who tried to break into our house and hurt us while we were away in Vancouver for the summer has become a fading memory. But later that year, I learn what the word bastard actually means.

And then I feel stunned.

My mom wasn't married to the man who got her pregnant while she was still married to my dad, so I guess the baby who was born a year before I was born is a bastard. I feel bad for thinking about the baby while using that word and I feel guilty and then sad all over again. I want to meet the baby, who would now be nine I guess, but none of us know where he is. I don't know if the baby, who is now no longer a baby, still has the name my mom and dad gave him before they gave him up for adoption when he was a week old and when my dad realized he couldn't bring himself to raise a child who was not his own. Maybe one day, I think to myself, I will be able to meet my brother and find out if he still has the same name. So I make up an imaginary friend and give him that name. And I play with my imaginary friend sometimes, in the basement, where it's cool, and I lie down on the concrete floor and race my miniature sports cars back and forth.

And maybe that's why, even though my mom and dad had me a year later and I wasn't a bastard, they eventually *got separated*.

After my day of activities at the YMHA, where I don't end up telling Leah about my half brother because she is busy telling me that soon she is going to get a new baby sister, because her parents, who are still married to each other, are adopting one, I head down to the basement in my house.

I pause on the stairs and try to recall exactly where the blood spots were. Then I walk all the way down and rummage through my toys and games to find my soccer ball. I give it a couple of bounces and ask my imaginary friend with the same name my mom and dad gave him nine years ago if he'd like to play.

CHAPTER 3

Fallujah

1992

They call the fields Fallujah. I know enough to know that with its "j sound" and opening letter "f," the word Fallujah is Arabic, not Hebrew, but I don't probe. I'm just glad to have been inducted into this little Labor Zionist community in Israel, this kibbutz in the desert, close enough to the Gaza Strip to be aware of the political tensions, and enough of an insider in this little community to know the nickname of the fields that some of the kibbutzniks drive to each morning, but far enough away to let my shoulders settle into the hot, dry embrace of the Negev.

Hebrew has always held a special place for me. When I was growing up, my dad's attention was sometimes hard to capture. He had moved out of my mom's house when I wasn't even yet four, and while I visited him regularly, the separation still stung. In our conversations, he often seemed tuned out. He claimed he had an active mental life. Maybe it was unacknowledged depression. But my dad was always alert when we were talking Hebrew. While I was away at Hebrew summer camp, he wrote me letters in Hebrew. Once I realized how rare this level of Hebrew knowledge was among ordinary Diaspora Jews, I felt superior. It wasn't so much my dad who incited this feeling of comparison—he wasn't particularly competitive and seemed to be secure in his Jewish identity. But it was a convenient way for me to mentally defend my flank against those who might, consciously or inadvertently, remind me of my gaps in Jewish belonging. My parents' marriage failed before that of any other Jewish

© The Author(s) 2021   37
M. Sucharov, *Borders and Belonging: A Memoir*,
https://doi.org/10.1007/978-3-030-53732-6_3

couples I knew, and then they both married non-Jewish spouses. Our record of synagogue membership was spotty and, despite my own Jewish day school attendance through grade 7 at least, and my own active Jewish youth group leadership roles, neither of my parents engaged in weekly Judaic rituals like Shabbat dinner. When my dad met my future stepmom, when I was ten, he and I stopped speaking Hebrew together. She didn't know the language and felt excluded.

Here in Israel, Hebrew candy and street names and pop songs and pizza toppings and the basic laws of the Knesset still elicit a rush of emotion in me. It's as if I'm back chatting in Hebrew with my dad. Or back at Hebrew summer camp. Except here it has the gravity of real life: the kind that doesn't end as the summer wanes and campers pack up their duffel bags to return to their waiting bedrooms, newly organized and dusted. The kind of real life where speaking Hebrew isn't merely a fun pastime to signal shared heritage and identity; it's the language in which residents eat, work, argue, and dream.

Every other weekend, when classes end at the Hebrew University on Mount Scopus, I take the bus to this kibbutz from Jerusalem, then another from Be'er Sheva, where I wait in the small bus station for my connection, the sidewalk flecked with bits of chewing gum and the smells of shwarma and falafel and hot garbage wafting by.

The kibbutz, made up of 120 families, making it small-to-mid-sized, has created a student program for us. *Studentim*, we're called. There are around a dozen of us, Americans and Canadians. We're assigned work branches and are known as "corks," filling in wherever there is a last-minute need, despite our protestations to the work roster coordinator. We tell him that we have definite preferences: wiping tables down in the dining hall is low on our wish list; heavy manual labor, where we can really feel part of the pioneering spirit, is higher. I like painting beams in the metal shop and taking breaks with the other workers, all kibbutzniks except for Moti who comes in every day from the nearby town to work. They are almost all men two decades my senior, and we enjoy snacking on plates of hot toast and sweet tea served in glass cups.

The kibbutz has provided the expats with a spacious apartment to share, and we each have been assigned a kibbutz family. Mine consists of a mom and dad in their forties, and their three kids: two sons, aged four and seven, and a daughter, aged twelve. The daughter is mostly distracted with her own preteen life: her friends, her schoolwork, and her main passion—the horses in the stables a few hundred yards away.

The brothers, though, take an immediate liking to me. I play soccer in the yard with them, and I read them bedtime stories plucked from their bedroom shelf filled with Hebrew picture books. It doesn't take long for me to forge a loving connection with them as I have with my own, much younger cousins back in Canada. Sometimes, on the bus ride from Be'er Sheva, I sit with a soldier, someone from the kibbutz who I recognize, and who is coming home for the weekend. These soldiers are around our age, and despite our daily activities being as different as they can be—me in classes on Mount Scopus and them guarding their base or patrolling a refugee camp or manning a checkpoint or completing grueling hikes, we soon develop an easy rapport. But the Intifada is still going on and I make sure to avoid asking too many questions about what they actually do. I picture them harassing Palestinian families in the middle of the night and then quickly shove the images from my mind.

As the kibbutz fields come into view through the windows of the bus, I finish the last few bites of my Pesek Z'man candy bar. *Pesek Z'man*, meaning Time Out, is like a Kit Kat, only creamier. Along with chocolate rugelach and chocolate Elite candy bars with pop rocks embedded in them, it's one of my favorite snacks this year in Israel.

As I disembark, I scan the area for kibbutzniks I know. I'm a bit disappointed and a bit relieved to see no one I recognize. A few months earlier, I had fallen for a cute paratrooper reservist named Gitai. I am constantly on the lookout for him, half-hoping he might acknowledge me, half-knowing he won't.

I stuff the shiny candy wrapper into the pocket of my jeans as I sling my green backpack with its Canadian flag over my shoulder. The lore from backpackers in Europe and the broader Middle East is that tourists are safer with a Canadian flag. Israelis don't seem to care either way— being Jewish from anywhere is generally the ticket to acceptance, but the Canadian flag is handy when I'm traveling elsewhere this year, in France, Switzerland, and Egypt, during university school breaks. The world seems to love Canada. "Canada Dry!" the Egyptian shopkeepers call out to us on the streets of Cairo as we pass by them.

Whenever I arrive at the kibbutz—every other weekend or so—my senses brace for a tingling overload. The sweet microbes that rush my nose from the piles of manure in the cowshed not far from the main gate. The dry heat of the desert, escapable easily enough in the air-conditioned dining hall or under the shade of one of the giant palm trees that grace the main lawn. The understated beauty of the cacti that press their vitality into the desert landscape alongside clusters of purple anemones. The fields of red poppies that flood the surrounding wadi whenever winter gives way to spring. The softness of the pink kibbutz factory blankets we've been issued for the beds in our student apartment with its pecan tree-shaded patio, and the dirt that lodges under my finger-nails as I sort potatoes on a combine. The sound of the toaster spitting out thin slices of bread, signaling that our morning tea break at the metal shop has begun. The boisterous kids and their gregarious parents and the tangy labneh spread on sticky yeast buns at Friday lunch, and the strap-ping soldiers and reservists whose attention we compete for at the Friday night disco.

I love kibbutz. I love everything about it. I love that I feel physically safe: no robbers, no cars, no bus bombs. I love that I feel seen. I love that I can know people and they can know me and it is like my own mini universe. I love the basketball court and the dining hall and the shady spots under the trees. I love that I can have a few drinks at the disco and not worry about how I'll get home. I love befriending Israelis and feeling like I am part of something that isn't quite mine. It reminds me of camp: a little self-enclosed universe where everything is in Hebrew.

But I have never asked why the kibbutzniks call the nearby agricultural fields by the Arabic name: Fallujah.

The other fields, the ones closer to the perimeter of the kibbutz, make me woozy with pioneering longings. One afternoon, I stand on a combine, sorting potatoes from the red earth with my friend Jen, another North American. As the potatoes pass by me on the conveyer belt, I am saying "potato, potato, potato, potato," and making Jen crack up. I am trying to parody the monotony of the job, but really I am totally stoked to be on this combine at this moment in the hot sun sorting potatoes and living what I think is the pioneering Labor Zionist dream of "Jewry of Muscle" that Zionist philosopher Max Nordau wrote about.

As the bus pulls away, I head toward my kibbutz family's house at the other end of the lawn and soon spot my kibbutz "brother" approaching on his bike. "*Ahlan*, Mira!" he shouts, using the Arabic-Hebrew slang for *hey*. I give him a high five. "Mah nishma?" I have to stop myself from squeezing his small shoulders. I want to respect his space. He hops expertly off his bike and walks it, so I can keep up. I follow him along the sidewalks that snake through the well-tended gardens toward his house at the other end of the perimeter road. There's still a couple of hours before Shabbat starts and I'll welcome the chance to sit and have a cup of tea with spearmint plucked fresh from my kibbutz mom's garden. I need some help planning my Israeli foreign policy term paper. Maybe they'll have some ideas.

But my mind is on Gitai. Things with him had started off on a kind of roller coaster. Gitai and I had hung out together on a trip the kibbutz hosted for the North American students and the kibbutzniks roughly our age. The kibbutzniks showed us how to make coffee in the brush and how to ride an inner tube down the Jordan, and we showed them how to ice skate in a community center named for a group of Canadian donors. My eyes were on Gitai.

While most of the kibbutznik work is done nearby, either in the surrounding potato fields, the blanket factory, the cowshed, dining hall, preschool, or laundry, Gitai would join a small cadre of members every morning to drive fifty-five kilometers to the Fallujah fields that the kibbutz had acquired for farming.

Back at the Hebrew University, my American friends and I joke about Gitai's name, which comes from the Hebrew word *gat*, a wine press. The agricultural resonance made us realize what Labor Zionism looks like when it decides to dress up in the form of an overseas student's kibbutz crush. "Do you want him to press *your* grapes?" my friend asks me, as we collapse into laughter.

Soon enough, I phoned my boyfriend back at McGill.

"I want my freedom," I told him on a long-distance phone call from the group pay phone in the dorms.

He wasn't happy about this. "What the hell do you mean, your freedom? You feel like our relationship is like being in fucking jail?"

I glanced behind me as the line got longer. "I just mean that I want a little more, uh, latitude. To get the whole, you know, Israel experience." I cringed as I said it.

"You're being selfish," he said.

"I'm not being selfish," I insisted. "You can still visit me at reading week. We can hang out. I'll show you around. But we should be free agents."

"I don't want to be a free agent!"

Finally, I pulled out the phone card and retreated back to my room, feeling guilty and defensive, until I realized that maybe I *was* being selfish. And maybe that was okay. Maybe looking out for my desires and preferences more than for those of my boyfriend back in Canada was part of the Israel experience I was supposed to have this year.

Figuring Gitai and I were now in the about-to-become-a-couple stage, the next time I was on the kibbutz I decided to show up unannounced at his apartment door. I knocked.

After a few seconds, he opened it.

"Hi," he said.

"Hi," I said. And then my smile faded. Over his left shoulder I could see a woman I didn't recognize. He introduced me but didn't invite me in. I stood on the threshold, shifting from foot to foot, bewildered and embarrassed.

So I did what I do when I'm trying to act cool in Israel and that is to begin talking rapidly. In Hebrew. I told them how much I'd been struggling with my Arabic class, which was being taught in Hebrew and entailed translating newspaper articles—"I don't even know how to say Molotov cocktail in Hebrew, never mind in Arabic," I said, trying out some Intifada humor—and "thank goodness I've found an Israeli study partner who is really patient. Maybe I'll see you guys later at the disco," I managed. And then I closed the door and walked back to my kibbutz family's house for dinner, my stomach lurching with rejection.

Over at my kibbutz family's house, we ate a meal of scrambled eggs, Israeli salad, cottage cheese, and sliced challah—and then I played a round of monopoly with my kibbutz brothers. But my heart wasn't in it.

I returned to my apartment, opened the door, and heard the echo of my footsteps on the Jerusalem tile. It was empty. All the other students must still be with their kibbutz families, I figured. I lay facedown on my bed, trying to catch a few minutes of an avoidance nap, clutching the pink kibbutz factory comforter to my cheek—when I heard a knock at the door. *That's strange*, I thought—we rarely got knocks. In our student pad, people generally came and went as they pleased.

When I opened the door, my heart leapt. Standing there was Gitai. This time I waited for him to speak. He told me that the woman in his room was just a friend. Well, they dated for a bit last year, he admitted, at the university in Be'er Sheva. And she'd like to start up again. But he's not interested, he assured me. And I decided to believe him.

I no longer felt I needed to resort to rapid Hebrew to fill the silence. He smiled as he licked the corner of his lip and asked me if I felt like heading over to the disco. Or maybe we should just skip the disco, he added, and go back to his room and listen to the new R.E.M. album. It's called *Automatic for the People*, he said, and it's amazing.

But now, with my kibbutz brother as cover, I can glance around the area feeling less alone and thus less self-conscious. I'm a bit relieved that Gitai is nowhere in sight. If he were to pass by as I'm walking alone, I know I'd hope that he'd want to stop and have a conversation; I know I'd hope that I might still be interesting enough to him. But I know that he wouldn't stop; walking with my kibbutz brother keeps my eyes and heart focused on the links I do have rather than searching for connections that have disappeared.

Not long after our R.E.M. listening session, I phoned Gitai. I was in my dorm room in Jerusalem. He was in his student apartment in Be'er Sheva. As our stilted conversation wound down into awkward silence, he spoke. "I guess I'll see you when I see you," he said. "Yeah, I guess." And my heart sank.

My kibbutz brother and I arrive at his house, where his little brother is waiting for us. I give them both a proper hug and turn to my kibbutz parents and embrace them too. It feels good to be back.

Eventually, when I am in my thirties and with kids of my own, I will sit at the cafeteria tables at the Jewish Community Centre in Ottawa, drinking weak coffee and chipping away at a research article on my laptop while my kids are in preschool downstairs. I will write an essay on Palestinian memory, and I will click on the newsletter of Zochrot, an Israeli NGO whose mission it is to get Israelis to think more about the Nakba. Part of how the group does this is by placing signs around Israeli towns and cities, marking the original Palestinian villages that are now no more, their inhabitants having fled or been expelled in 1948. In the newsletter I will read an interview with one of the founders, an Israeli Jewish citizen named Eitan Bronstein.

I will be curious, but I will also flinch. I love the name Eitan. It means soundness, steadiness. But the oddly articulated grammar of the word *zochrot*—the unusual ending where normally the word would be *zikaron* (memory), *zichronot* (memories) or *zachor* (remember) is meant to lodge in the throat while also evoking a progressive, feminine twist. But I will push all that away, thinking it a bit too calculated. Plus I'm suspicious of the anti-Zionist agenda of Zochrot. It's a bridge too far for me. When it comes to the refugees, what's done is done, I will think. Better to focus on a two-state solution, better to think about helping push for Israel to withdraw from the West Bank, making way for Palestinian sovereignty there, rather than try to roll back Zionist history altogether.

Several years after that, once I've encountered more scholars and friends whose sympathies extend far beyond my liberal Zionist bubble to embrace those who have been victimized by it, once I've been comfortably teaching the material to my students in a way that feels emotionally safe enough for me to wonder whether there's deeper, more ethical questioning to be done, I will struggle. My mind will drift back to my time on kibbutz and to the little clues of erased Palestinian history that were obviously not fully erased. The kibbutzniks could have called those fields by the region's Hebrew name—which also happens to be Eitan—but there was evidently something appealing to them about using the Arabic name, Fallujah.

Why did they call it Fallujah, given that so much of Israeli culture has involved Hebraicizing names—names of people and names of places? I will begin to wonder whether it represents a perverse mix of affection or a linguistic souvenir from a trophy hunt. But then I will feel guilty for even imagining that ugly metaphor—a trophy hunt—so I'll swat that thought away too.

This year, 1992, at Hebrew University, I've been much more interested in the Palestinians in the West Bank and Gaza, if I think of them at all. The "Arab Israelis," as they are known in our circles, seem like a less sexy topic. A less urgent policy issue. They have citizenship. The Palestinians in the West Bank and Gaza, on the other hand, are under occupation. What I don't yet fully realize is that many of the Palestinians in the West Bank and most of the Palestinians in Gaza started out in what I now think of as Israel proper.

My interest in the occupation has been long-standing. On the way to my year of adventure this year, I brought along David Grossman's *The Yellow Wind*, a journalistic account of Palestinian life in the occupied territories, to read on the plane. Another Canadian student on the flight, walking up and down the aisles, stretching, said "I like your book," leaning in to get a better look at the cover. We introduced ourselves. She was from Toronto, studying at McGill like me. We decided to be roommates in the Jerusalem dorms.

Decades later, when I'm a professor and columnist for Israeli and other Jewish papers, and whose work usually fits quite squarely within the liberal Zionist consensus but who starts to feel pangs of doubt and curiosity about the layers of Palestinian history that have been mostly shunted aside in my consciousness, I won't be able to push the thoughts of Fallujah away altogether. So I will investigate a little further and discover that Al-Fallujah was the name of the Palestinian village conquered by Israeli forces in 1949. During the Battle of Be'er Sheva in 1948, it became known as the Fallujah Pocket. I will read more about Fallujah on the website of Zochrot. In 1948, the village had a population of 5420. I don't know where all the survivors of the war ended up, but I suspect many of them fled to Gaza nearby, joining the other thousands of Palestinian refugees in the tiny strip.

I keep searching. I will find *The Palestine Remembered* website, and, clicking to its entry on Fallujah, I will get a chill. The village, it says, was "ethnically cleansed" 25,358 days ago, when Israeli forces occupied it on March 1, 1949. I do a quick calculation. When Gitai and I were listening to *Automatic for the People*, the count was 15,928 days. To most Palestinians and to many solidarity activists, of course, each day that is added to the automated calendar-counter is one more reminder that their challenge of refugee return still awaits. By the time I'm revising this book manuscript a final time, another six-hundred days will have been added.

The morning after we listened to that album, Gitai returned to Fallujah, while I took my leave back to Jerusalem, hoping to see him again the following week and wondering how much he wanted the same. I was quickly realizing that my infatuation with him—his Israeli coolness, his muscular frame, his charming aloofness—was no match for his feeling that I, in my North American-Jewish visitor-to-his-kibbutz persona, was just one of many. There would be more where I came from, just as there had been in previous years: other long curly-haired, sun-kissed women who shed their Canadian sweaters for borrowed kibbutz work clothes on Friday mornings, and who changed out of those work clothes on Friday nights, into jeans and a tight T-shirt to gather at the kibbutz disco in an old community hall between the cowshed and the blanket factory, to flirt in Hebrew and drink rum and Pepsi and dance to Ace of Bass. Some of those women from past youth movement delegations who had caught Gitai's eye I could even list by name. One was even among my closest friends. A month earlier, I had sent her a blue aerogram, filling the pages with descriptions of my activities and longings, and asking her permission to pursue Gitai, one of the guys she'd left behind. "Enjoy. Have all the best experiences," she'd written back.

One of these villagers from Fallujah, I learn by reading an article about the displacement published on the al-Jazeera news site, is named Umm Omar, Omar's mom. She was eight years old at the time of the attacks, the same age as Lior, my kibbutz brother, the year I spent on the kibbutz. If she is now in her mid-seventies, her son Omar is probably around my age. This would mean that he has no direct memories of Fallujah. He would have been born in Gaza, likely in the refugee camp Jabaliya, where his mother still lives, fifteen miles from the kibbutz where I slept under pink blankets and spent afternoons alongside the pecan tree.

My time on that kibbutz, not far from Fallujah, felt ordained. Living out a sense of pioneering Labor Zionist history was the closest thing I'd had, since my Bat Mitzvah, to an authentic spiritual experience—though one tied more to ethnicity and a sense of collective memory than to God or formal religion. But that sense of transcendence came close, on occasion, to morphing into dogmatism.

Early on in the year, I was working in the kibbutz preschool. One kid, blonde, around three years old, came in clutching a picture book he'd brought from home. His dad was one of our work coordinators and we were pretty friendly. But that morning I was all business. I told this child clearly and directly that he must leave his book in his cubby for the day. Only communal property was allowed, and this book, brought only by him to be kept by him, was, in my view, contraband. It violated the basic tenets of kibbutz socialist philosophy. He screamed and cried but I stood firm.

It was the only thing I did that year that I fully regret. I had become a zealot.

I should have known better. I, too, had a transitional object I treasured at that age. In the house with the hardwood floors and screened-in front porch, I had a pink blanket—two shades darker than the ones they would give us on kibbutz, years later. This one was lined with tiny indentations and edged with two inches of pink satin all around. I carried that blanket back and forth across those hardwood floors. My blanket had special powers. Up and down, moving the blanket a centimeter at a time across my face, I believed I could detect distinct scents. The flowery smell. The sour smell. The stinky smell. The sweet smell.

Later in the year I was working in the kibbutz laundry. My short-lived relationship with Gitai had come to an end some months earlier and I still felt pangs of longing. That day in the laundry, as my friend's kibbutz mom passed me a pile of shirts to fold, I spotted Gitai's laundry number on the inside collar of a blue work shirt. On the kibbutz, every household has a dedicated laundry number stamped on a cloth tag that the sewing shop affixes to each item of clothing so that the laundry workers know where to distribute the clean clothes. If ever I had laundry that I didn't take back with me to Jerusalem, I could use my kibbutz family's code. By then, I had also memorized Gitai's three-digit number. I felt a familiar rush of excitement followed by a twinge of embarrassment that I was thrust into this bit of domestic intimacy in the midst of daily kibbutz life. I was reminded that I still found him, or at least the idea of him, alluring, while he probably never gave me a second thought.

I was partly in this community and partly outside of it. This community was both mine and not mine. This community was one we joined on Shavuot, sitting on haystacks and wearing kibbutz trucker hats along with the kibbutzniks and taking in the ceremonial showcase of the annual yield: of plants, of calves, of babies.

That year I had never asked why the kibbutzniks called the area by its Arabic name. Instead, I had savored the remaining bites of my Israeli candy bar called "time out," because that's exactly what I needed after a long week of classes at the Hebrew University. Plus, things were waiting for me: the spearmint in my kibbutz mom's garden and the chicken soup in the kibbutz dining hall, and the fallen pecans on our apartment patio, and the Friday night kibbutz disco—with my American friends and the attractive soldiers and reservists and the sounds of Ace of Base and Snow and Haddaway. I brought my collection of shekels. Three shekels for a rum and Pepsi from the curly-haired bartender with a kind face and brown eyes. The shekels were as thick as nickels but smaller than dimes. They felt good in my hand. I brought nine: enough for three drinks. Always rum and Pepsi.

Over the next twenty-five years, I will visit my kibbutz family many times in Israel. They will soon leave the kibbutz for another kibbutz where they can own their house and be financially independent. They will visit my husband and I in Washington DC, in Vancouver, and twice in Ottawa, where we will now have kids of our own. They won't judge me and my increasingly "leftist" politics. They will contact me by Facetime on my birthday, and through the camera on my phone, I will show them our garden, the lawn dried out from the south-facing sun. I will love them and they will love me. And when I visit them on their new kibbutz, they will give me the fortified room to sleep in when things heat up at the Gaza border, a kilometer away, so that if the sirens go off in the middle of the night, I can stay where I am, and they will come to me.

And years after that, I will be listening to seventies Israeli rock on a loop in my car as I drive to pick up my kids. "How was Hebrew school?"

I'll ask on the ride home, passing the Ottawa experimental farm on our left. The strawberry stands on the side of the road are just beginning to open and I will look over with a flicker of longing before deciding to go straight home. It's been a long day. In answer to my question, the kids will mumble something about being happy it's over.

"You've learned a lot about Israel, right? Now I'd like to tell you a bit about the Palestinians," I will say, while the seventies Israeli rock continues in the background.

"Hey Yo Ya, I ask; Hey Yo Ya, you answer."

I will teach my kids a bit about checkpoints and the occupation. In Hebrew. Which is what I speak to them all the time, even when my daughter was fourteen months old and in the hospital one night, her diaper bone-dry from a urinary tract infection, and I was trying to soothe her. I speak only Hebrew to them, enjoying our private language in public places, our secret code; unless someone we know is around who doesn't understand the language and would feel excluded, and then I switch to English to be polite.

CHAPTER 4

Re/Intermarriage

1980

I'm running my hands along my birthday soccer ball, which I've had for
a couple of weeks and which I'll have to leave at home in July because
I'm getting ready to go away to summer camp and there won't be room
for it in my duffel bag. This camp is not the one I really want to go to.
The one I really want to go to is the Jewish camp my dad went to for
thirteen summers, the camp where everyone speaks Hebrew.

"Oh, Maccabiah. I *loved* Maccabiah," my dad told me one night, when
I was five. I was brushing my teeth in his apartment bathroom, still in my
bathing suit from the pool. The black and orange remnants of the tiger-
tail ice cream I'd eaten that afternoon were running down my chin into
the sink.

After I changed into my pajamas, my dad came into my room and
tucked me into bed, telling me about the Alice-in-Wonderland themed
meal his Maccabiah team had designed when he was a teenager. He
explained that when he was a kid it was the *nineteen-fifties* and the *Alice*
Disney movie had just come out. A decade later, it was cool for the
teens—him and the other counselors—to look back on the story and the
movie they had grown up with.

"We decorated the *chadar ochel* with giant playing cards and red and
white roses," he said. "The campers dressed up as the characters from
Alice in Wonderland. There was Alice of course, plus the Cheshire Cat,
Tweedledum and Tweedledee, and the Queen of Hearts. And we played

© The Author(s) 2021
M. Sucharov, *Borders and Belonging: A Memoir*,
https://doi.org/10.1007/978-3-030-53732-6_4

hedgehog croquet with flamingo mallets that the counselors made out of cardboard."

My eyes widened. I pictured summer camp scenes rolling by in cartoon style. I had seen the movie too, with my dad.

But I can't go to that Hebrew camp yet because you have to be nine. So this year, when I'm eight, I go to the YMCA camp instead. The lake is pretty and there are bonfires and marshmallows and we swim and canoe and wear ponchos when it rains. In art, we make pendants out of a slice of tree branch that we varnish and then hang around our necks from a string of yarn. But I don't know anyone in my cabin from school because it's not a Jewish camp, and the school I go to is a Jewish school. Most of the Jewish kids are waiting until they are nine to go to camp. But I heard my mom tell Ron, her boyfriend, that I should go to camp this year, because they need time for *wedding planning*. So I go to sleep each night at this non-Jewish camp, in a cabin surrounded by kids I don't know, with swirls in my stomach.

When the bus deposits me back in Winnipeg at the end of the session, I walk down the steps and enjoy the feel of asphalt underfoot. I'm crying a little because I'm still sort of homesick even though I'm back home, so I pull my baseball cap down over my face so no one will see my eyes.

"Mertz!" I hear Ron's voice. "I barely saw you with your hat pulled down. C'mere!" He pulls me towards him and gives me a hug.

Ron has brought along his youngest child, Stevie, to pick me up. I'm confused about whether to be happy or sad about the reason for Stevie being in Winnipeg this week: he's here, visiting from Edmonton, because my mom and his dad are getting married. And once they get married, we might have to move to a bigger house because Ron's three oldest kids— Stevie's two sisters and his older brother—might come to live with us. And if we move to a bigger house, we'll probably have to move to the north end, where houses are cheaper, my mom explains, and that means that I'll have to start a new school. At least it will still be a Jewish school.

Stevie is older and cooler than me and he's pretty cute, from the pictures I've seen, mostly the one of Ron's four kids that sits on top of our piano. They look like Brady Bunch kids, except there are two boys and two girls, instead of three of each. There's another picture of another one of Ron's kids—an additional stepbrother I would have had—but he died before I was born, of leukemia, when he was three and a half. In the photo, he is wearing a tiny blazer and bow tie. Whenever I walk from the living room to my bedroom, rounding the corner past my mom's and Ron's room, I glance at the photo and feel a bit sad and curious and affectionate and guilty for being alive when he's not.

When I complain to my mom that Ron's kids don't pay much attention to me, she explains that they're jealous.

My brow furrows. They are older and smarter than me. Some even go to university. Some even have *jobs*. One works at Safeway and another works at the *Re-Man* center, where, I figure, criminals go to learn how to become *real men* again. How can *they* be jealous of *me*?

"It's because you get to live with their dad and they don't," my mom says.

I shrug. I miss living with my dad too. But I don't say that aloud.

Visiting my dad at his house is okay. There's wall-to-wall cream carpet that goes on forever. There's a brick wall in the back lane where I can play 7-Up with a tennis ball. And there's a Betamax. My dad likes to show me old movies that he rents at Advance Video or Adi's Video or records right from the TV. *The Jazz Singer* with Al Jolson. *A Christmas Carol. The Man in the Glass Booth.* The first and third ones are Jewish. And *The Man in the Glass Booth* has something to do with the Holocaust, but I'm not exactly sure what.

The Betamax has a control attached to the TV by a long cord that can make a scene go in slow motion if you adjust a round dial, or show it frame by frame if you press a tiny rectangular button. Once, when we were watching *Kramer vs. Kramer*, my dad showed me how the director created the scene where Billy falls off the monkey bars while holding his toy airplane and cuts his lip. In one frame, his face is fine. In the next, it's bloody. In between those two frames, my dad explains, the crew stopped filming and applied fake blood to Billy's lip. My dad's explanation makes me feel a bit better about watching that scene. And I like knowing which actors are Jewish. My dad tells me that Dustin Hoffman, who plays Billy's dad, is.

The part of the movie that makes me saddest is the part that has no special effects. It's the part where Billy's parents *get separated*. And the scene that makes me really the most sad is when Billy's dad gets mad at him for taking ice cream he wasn't supposed to take, and his dad yells at him and carries him to his room. I figure the dad would be less mad if the mom was still around, and Billy would maybe behave better if his mom and dad still lived together. Whenever I watch that scene I feel lonely.

On Wednesday nights my dad takes me to dinner at Bonanza, where I always order the marinated chicken with French fries and salad bar. I like the sweet corn salad and the iceberg lettuce that sprays water into my mouth and which I cover with French dressing. After Bonanza, sometimes my dad tucks me into bed back at my mom's. One day I ask him for suggestions of topics to discuss in Hebrew class. Our teacher asked us to bring ideas. My dad suggests Jewish intellectuals, like Sigmund Freud and Albert Einstein. I know who Einstein is of course, and I already know a bit about Sigmund Freud because my dad is a psychiatrist. So the next day I suggest that, and my teacher praises me for such a grand topic. The day after that, I walk around my class asking my classmates if they know what *narcissistic rage* is. No, they say, and I don't offer any definition; I just nod sagely.

My dad's girlfriend, who lives in his apartment too but isn't around much when I'm there, collects Donald Duck and Scrooge and Archie comics, and I get a little shiver whenever I glance over into the corner where her comic books are stacked high. I don't ever touch them and she doesn't offer to lend them to me. I have my own supply of Betty and Veronica and Jughead digests.

My dad's girlfriend doesn't pay much attention to me. I prefer it when we visit her parents' house. There, she has a younger brother who is still a teenager and he has a cool name and an Apple computer with games you can play. I've never seen an Apple computer before. I look down at my digital watch with the tiny light I can turn on by pressing the button on the side, and compare it to this big machine with its colorful apple logo with rainbow stripes. Their mother makes macramé hanging plant holders. I've never met a grown-up who does arts and crafts just because they like to.

Maybe the reason my dad's girlfriend doesn't pay much attention to me is because she's jealous, the way my mom claims that Ron's kids are. But I can't understand why she would be. She gets to live with my dad, and I don't.

On Sunday afternoons I visit my dad at his apartment but I hardly ever sleep there. The last time I did sleep over, my dad took a bath and I was all by myself in the living room and I wanted someone to talk to so I went into the bathroom to find him but he told me to please give him *some privacy* and that hurt my feelings.

My dad's girlfriend has a nickname for me: Miroslav. Usually my dad calls me Mirtz or Mirtzos, which I like. But sometimes he copies what his girlfriend says and calls me Miroslav, and then they both say that I'm *a riot* or *a scream*. I don't like being called any of those things. I never say anything about it, though.

"Is this your bag?" Ron examines the label of a navy duffel bag sitting in the pile of camp luggage. My duffel has no zipper, only metal holes where a string scrunches it all up, forming a sausage-shaped package. I worked hard to stuff everything in when I packed to come home. My sleeping bag at the bottom, then my pillow, then my sheets and towels, then my rain boots, poncho, and sandals, and finally my clothes.

I nod, and follow along behind Stevie.

"How was camp, Mertz?" Ron opens the car door and leans the driver's seat forward so I can climb into the back seat. I clip the ends of the seat belt together across my lap. The plush seat is soft under my legs. I run my hand along it in each direction. Stevie gets to sit in the front because he's already a teenager.

"Camp was okay." I'm still blinking back tears, thinking about being homesick. I don't want to cry in front of Stevie. Ron starts the ignition and we drive home, back to my room with my Judy Blume books and my Mr. Merlin electronic game and my mini baseball bats engraved with Pete Rose's autograph. The baseball bats I got in the mail when I sent away for things from the book called *Free Stuff for Kids*. To get the free stuff, we had to write a business letter to the company and include our return address. Maybe I'll look for more free stuff to send away for this week, before school starts.

Ron not being Jewish means that we get to teach him the *hamotzi*. "Do the *hamotzi*!" I prod him, when my aunt, uncle, and grandmother are over.

"OK," he says. "Here goes. *Baruch atah adonai, eloheinu melech ha'olam, ha-motzi lechem mean ha'aretz.*" As he says *lechem* it sounds like he's bringing everything up from his throat. We all laugh appreciatively.

Ron not being Jewish also means that he brought a box to our basement filled with something I'd only seen in movies: Christmas lights. They never do get hung around our house. But in third grade, I go down to the basement and select a single red bulb to use for my science project. Inside the papier-mâché volcano I've built, and alongside the columns of information I've copied, word for word, from the encyclopedia entry "Volcanoes and Geysers," I place the bulb, connected to its plastic-encased wires, inside the volcano as smoke emerges from the block of dry ice Ron brought home for me one afternoon.

The following year, for my science project on light and color, I pick out four lights: red, blue, green, and yellow, and put three Rubik's cubes in three boxes with a peephole cut out, in front of each bulb. By now I know you're not supposed to copy from an encyclopedia word for word. For this project, my dad builds me a three-paneled backboard out of plywood secured with tiny brass hinges. Onto the backboard I paste colored sheets of paper from my great-uncle's printing company and on the top of each I use Letraset to affix the titles. *Problem. Background. Discussion.*

At the wedding, there are platters filled with hors d'oeuvres and fruit punch for kids and grown-up punch for grown-ups. There is Pepsi, Ron's favorite drink. Ron doesn't drink alcohol because he's Baptist. But he does like to play cards and he teaches me how to play Cribbage and even how to keep score with the tiny pegs.

Since it's an *intermarriage*, my mom couldn't find a rabbi to conduct the wedding. So instead she picked a judge who is Jewish. He has gray hair and an official-looking robe. We pose for photographs next to the giant green plants and big pink flowers in the park's conservatory. But the photo shoot and the pretty plants and my custom-made dress with spaghetti straps and eyelet fabric, and the tasty hors d'oeuvres, and the extra attention from my grandparents and my aunts and uncles aren't enough to push away all my topsy-turvy feelings. After all, my dad isn't invited, and most of all, my mom and Ron's wedding reminds me that my parents' *separation* is now permanent. At least next summer I'll be old enough to go to Hebrew summer camp. There, I won't have to think as much about the separation and who is Jewish and who isn't and who is jealous of who because someone gets to live with someone else's dad.

CHAPTER 5

Moles

1993

"Pancakes?" My mom is holding a spatula in one hand and reaching for the electric frying pan with the other. She cracks three eggs into a bowl, adds milk, and whisks. "Ron bought a flat of blueberries yesterday." She motions to the fridge and to my stepdad with a single wave of her arm. I open the fridge and grab a handful of the berries and pop them in my mouth. I feel the little spheres pop and savor them as I swallow. Israel easily wins on tomatoes and cucumbers, but nothing beats B.C. berries.

I've just returned from Winnipeg Beach, where I attended Hebrew summer camp as a member of the senior staff. I had flown to Winnipeg in July, straight from Israel, where my year as an overseas student at the Hebrew University of Jerusalem had just wrapped up. Now I have a week left in Vancouver to visit my family before I return to Montreal, to finish my degree at McGill. One more year and then I can return to Israel, hopefully to live in Tel Aviv this time and spend another year in the country working, before starting graduate school. I can't wait to get back.

Now that I'm in Canada, though, even digging into a bowl of Cheerios or mini shredded wheat is a kind of succor. There weren't many North American-style breakfast cereals to choose from in Israel. Israelis call every kind of cereal "cornflakes," an indication that the selection isn't vast. If you wanted actual juice, rather than a sugary juice-style beverage, you had to specify "natural juice." Coffee was instant unless you requested "filter."

© The Author(s) 2021
M. Sucharov, *Borders and Belonging: A Memoir*,
https://doi.org/10.1007/978-3-030-53732-6_5

Not that I drank coffee anyway. I preferred spearmint tea right from my kibbutz mom's garden.

My mom hands me a plate of pancakes. I pour maple syrup over them, cut a large wedge, and angle a forkful into my mouth. The *Vancouver Sun* is spread out across the table and I flip through it as I chew, my mind mostly on what awaits me back in Montreal: a cool apartment close to campus in the McGill ghetto and being reunited with Sandra, the flatmate I've missed while I was away. More Middle East Studies courses. And figuring out how to arrange some sort of work in Israel after I graduate.

I haven't read a Canadian newspaper in over a year. Sometimes we'd get the *International Herald Tribune* in Jerusalem. Flipping through the *Vancouver Sun* now feels both familiar and exotic. I linger on the lead headline. "Israel and PLO say historic deal imminent: Palestinian self-rule expected in troubled occupied territories." Reading the article, I discover that while I was living in Israel this past year, thinking almost nonstop about Israeli and Palestinian politics, Israeli government officials and high-level members of the PLO were negotiating, secretly, in Oslo, Norway. My mind flips back to just a couple of months ago when I managed to secure a short internship in the Knesset. Dressed in the most professional outfit I could muster from my duffel bags filled with university sweatshirts and kibbutz work clothes, I put on my white jeans and a burgundy silk blouse and brown leather sandals and strode up the long plaza, past the famous iron gates, toward the grand doors of the Knesset. And all this time, I now think to myself, a historic deal was being negotiated between Israel and the PLO and no one told me.

I wonder for a moment whether it would have been more momentous to have lived in Jerusalem in the first year of an Israeli–Palestinian peace deal, which would be this year, or in the final year of their pre-peace relationship, as I apparently did. In any event, when I return next year, it will still be the beginning stages of a new era of peace. This means that the Intifada will be over, and I'll be able to explore East Jerusalem. Maybe I'll even get to spend some time visiting Ramallah or Jericho and get to know Palestinian culture more in-depth.

We'll have a lot to talk about this fall in our Israeli–Arab dialogue group at McGill. I've been active in Israeli–Arab activities on campus since my first year. Being part of the Habonim crowd—my Labor Zionist youth group—and then co-president of PZC, Progressive Zionist Caucus, meant that I had older students around mentoring me, inspiring me to think about Middle East Politics in ways that felt both urgent and intimate. But sometimes real-life incidents over there, in Israel–Palestine, overwhelmed me here, in Canada, and I didn't have the political muscle to push my way through or the emotional compass to even read my own preferences.

One morning in October of my freshman year, the phone rang in my dorm room. I reached for the receiver; it was connected to the clock radio that the boys in my sixth-grade class had given my for my Bat Mitzvah. I glanced at the red digital numbers. 10:30 am. *Shit.* I'd slept through my morning class again.

"Hello?" I could hear the sleep in my voice.

"Hello Mira, it's Khaled," an unfamiliar voice said. He had an Arabic accent. "We met at the Arab-Jewish dialogue group last week. In the Arts building."

I did a mental scan of the students I had met that day. I could vaguely picture Khaled. He was a graduate student in computer science. Or maybe engineering. He had spoken up a lot at the meeting. I recalled that he was pleasant enough, but that I had also felt a bit put off by his intensity.

"I don't know if you've heard," Khaled said, "but things are very bad in Jerusalem."

"What do you mean?"

"Yesterday, the Israelis killed twenty Palestinians." He pronounced "Israelis" with four syllables, lingering on the first s.

Khaled explained that Israeli border police had shot Palestinian protesters around the Haram al-Sharif, the Temple Mount. "I'm hoping we can launch a response here at McGill," he said.

"Um, what do you have in mind?"

"A petition, a protest. Arab and Jewish students. Together. We must speak out against these atrocities committed by the Israeli state."

"I don't know if I..." I trailed off, winding the phone cord around my finger as I stared at the vintage Star Wars poster I'd taped to the back of my door.

A month earlier, I had gone shopping along Saint Catherine Street, in downtown Montreal, in search of decor for my dorm room. I found my way into a head shop. When my eyes landed on that Star Wars poster, I knew I had to have it. But then I spotted something else at the back of the store. It was a giant swastika flag. I weighed my options. I could walk out right now. I could protest. Or I could buy the poster and leave.

I screwed up my courage and approached the desk. "Excuse me," I said to the clerk, pointing to the wall. "That flag is really wrong."

"I'm not the manager," he said. He looked bored. "Besides, some customers like it. Collectors. Y'know, World War II memorabilia and all that."

I looked around the shop and saw no other customers, no collectors. And then I started to rationalize. As a Jew, I thought to myself, I was already hurt and offended by that swastika poster. Why should I have to suffer doubly by denying myself the purchase of the poster I wanted so badly? I looked from side to side. And then I carried the Star Wars poster to the counter, paid, and left, tucking the cardboard tube under my arm as I walked back uphill, the air still warm from summer, toward McConnell Hall.

That was the logic that led me to stare at the poster and twist the phone cord idly around my finger as an Arab student I had only met once asked me to organize a student-wide response to the Israeli border police killings. "I'm sorry to hear this news," I said. "It's very unfortunate. I'll talk to my friends. I'll get back to you." I hung up the phone and went back to sleep.

Although Montreal was over 2000 miles away from my home, I had planned on attending McGill as early as I can remember. In ninth grade, my uncle gave me a copy of Linda Frum's *Guide to Canadian Universities*. I devoured her cheeky descriptions of student life from coast to coast. McGill, with its fancy reputation mixed with black-clad sophisticates taking in the Montreal nightlife—seemed much more interesting to me than early nineties Vancouver. Vancouver was sushi and vegetarian noodle dishes and walks around the Stanley Park seawall. But Montreal offered another sort of pull altogether. Montreal was Mordecai Richler and Leonard Cohen and smoked meat you ordered no leaner than medium fat on rye, eating your sandwich and fries and drinking black cherry soda while your elbows grazed the diners beside you at Schwartz's Deli. Montreal was the Francophone-inflected club scene and repertory movie theaters and poutine and 24-hour Fairmont Bagels and Real Canadian Winters.

Plus, McGill was where my dad had gone, I'd tell people, when they asked how I had picked the university. As if that explained it. I knew nothing about legacy admissions. Not that Canadian universities had anything like that anyway, and not that I'd want to be associated with the worst kind of elitist practices like those, if I'd actually paused to consider them.

Until I arrived by airplane on Labor Day Weekend in 1990 to begin my degree, I had only visited Montreal once, when I was six. That summer, my dad had taken me to visit his old friends, the Finesilvers. As we descended over Quebec, I delighted in the art canvas that my airplane window had become, with tiny yellow lights dotting a midnight-blue background. I had flown to Vancouver before—for my aunt's wedding and to visit my grandparents—but I had never before flown at night.

On that trip, my dad took me to a fish hatchery outside the city, an attraction filled with concrete pools. When we deposited a nickel into a gumball-like machine, it spit out fish food pellets instead of candy. Clutching the food tightly, I approached the edge of the pool and tossed it in, mesmerized by the swarm of fish that bobbed to the surface to devour it. A month later, on a questionnaire our first-grade teacher handed us asking about our favorite things, next to "place" I wrote *Pissy Culture*, trying to render the unfamiliar French sound of the word *pisciculture* in my best approximation of consonants.

But my decision to move to downtown Montreal wasn't without its private terror. Nine months before I planned to set out for McGill, I'd been sitting in my dad and stepmom's kitchen when I heard the news: Marc Lépine had murdered fourteen women at the École Polytechnique. By all accounts, the massacre was motivated by misogyny of the worst and most terrifying kind. I tried to picture myself, an eighteen-year-old girl—I still didn't think of myself as a *woman*—walking the streets of Montreal. In my fantasies, the streets were always dark and deserted.

I shoved the Polytechnique murders out of my mind soon enough, though. Other friends from Vancouver were headed to McGill too, and we didn't talk much about the massacre, so I simply decided that I would not be scared.

And mostly I'm not scared, except when it's dark and I have to walk up the icy hill, past the Montreal Neurological Institute that no one ever seems to come in or out of, and toward my residence hall and my cinderblock-walled dorm room with my Mac SE and dot matrix printer and my kettle with mint tea and my bags of stale bagels leaning against a jar of peanut butter because there's no meal plan on weekends and we have to scrounge.

The Star Wars poster stares back at me, reminding me of my fair-weather ethics.

I finish my mom's pancakes just as I get to the end of the newspaper article about the peace deal. I flip the page. There, on the right-hand side, is an article about skin cancer. The article explains how to spot cancerous moles. The depleting ozone layer—and the attendant health risks—is on everyone's mind these days.

As I read the piece, my eyes wander down to my forearm, to a small mole staring back at me. Being larger than six mm in diameter—the size of a pencil eraser—is one of the warning signs, the article explains. This mole doesn't seem to be larger than six mm. But there *is* another warning sign—a dark spot in the middle. My face flushes. I look toward my mom and stepdad, who are playing Scrabble. "Mom, what do you think about this mole?" I show her my arm and then slide the newspaper toward her.

"Let's call your doctor and get it looked at."

A few days later, I am sitting in the doctor's office. I show her the mole. "It looks fine to me," she says. I hate needles and surgical procedures and try to savor the relief of avoiding the scalpel today. But something doesn't feel right.

"I think you should remove it and have it checked out," I say, inhaling.

"OK, I guess. If you really want it gone, I guess it can't hurt."

My doctor leaves the room and returns with a metal try filled with syringes and anesthetic and scalpels and gauze. A few minutes later, the mole is gone, and in its spot are three stitches covered by a small bandage.

A week later, I'm reading on the futon in my downtown Montreal apartment, in the neighborhood next to campus that everyone calls the McGill ghetto. The flat I share with Sandra has green-painted wooden floors in the front half, and checkered linoleum in the back. I have one more day to myself before classes start and I'm reading the latest Carol Shields novel, *The Stone Diaries*.

The phone rings. "Hi Mira, it's your Dad here."

"Hi Dad, how are you?"

"I'm okay," he says. His voice is focused and even.

"What's wrong?" I say. I still say "What's wrong?" even when nothing is wrong. It's become a reflex since moving away and worrying that every time my parents call me it's to relay some family disaster.

"The test results from your mole came back. You'll need to make an appointment with a plastic surgeon in Montreal to get more of the skin cells around the area removed."

My heart jumps as my pulse begins to race. "What do you mean? Why?"

"The results say that it is a marginally invasive melanoma." He speaks slowly, carefully enunciating the words.

Melanoma.

My eyes dart between my black-and-tan-striped duvet cover; and the *Rime of the Ancient Mariner* poster taped to the wall over my bed; and the bulletin board above my desk where I've tacked an Arabic fast-food chain menu from Cairo, a Hebrew bumper sticker from the Meretz party, and a few photos from camp this summer. Except for the time that I had a yeast infection and had to call the public health line and figure out how to say it in French—*champignons*, like mushrooms or fungus, the nurse explained—I've never had to get medical care in Montreal. I always just save my doctors' visits for check-ups when I'm back home. That's where my doctor is; that's where my dentist is; that's where home is.

"I'll call Goldberg," my dad says, referring to his old friend and classmate from medical school who is now a physician in Montreal. "I'm sure he'll have some advice about doctors you can consult with over there."

I hang up the phone as my eyes well up with tears. Sandra is out for the evening and suddenly I feel scared and completely alone. I let the tears flow as I dial my friend Amanda.

"Mands," I say, my voice breaking. "It's me. Mira."

"Hey Mirs, are you okay? What's happened?"

"I have melanoma." Now I'm really crying. "My dad called. I had a mole on my arm and I got it removed and the results came back cancerous and I'm really scared."

"I'll be right over," she says. "Let's go out tonight. I'm not letting you stay home alone being scared."

So we go out to a bar on St. Laurent. But the loud music and dim lighting and the sour smell of beer does nothing to distract me.

One week later, I'm in the office of the plastic surgeon who is going to carve up my arm. He is nearing retirement. He has a Jewish name. I think about other patients who have sat here, in this same office. Were they trying to smooth out a bumpy nose? Contemplating a face-lift? A breast reduction? Breast enhancement? Or were they staring death in the face with a recent diagnosis of skin cancer?

The surgeon tells me that I'm lucky. The cancer has been caught early.

"We will take out the cells we need to." He draws a quick diagram on a piece of paper, outlining a wide radius around the mole. He'll carve out as much as he needs and as little as possible, so that the margins are clean.

"What about the future, after the surgery? Do I need to make lifestyle changes?" I ask. This is all so new to me and I don't know where to begin.

I don't really know how to avoid the sun. The sun is everywhere. At least in the summer. And I can't remember tanning much since the afternoon in late June when our replacement seventh-grade Jewish day school teacher took a group of us to lie out at Kits Beach in Vancouver. We wore our Vuarnet sunglasses and Esprit shorts with rubber gummy bracelets that we called *gumi* bracelets, the Hebrew word for rubber. We'd heard that those bracelets—the black ones, at least—had come from Israeli army grenades. Sometimes I wore a fluorescent green one alongside my translucent Swatch watch where you could see all the moving gears, but mostly I liked the black bracelets because they seemed more authentic.

That afternoon at Kits Beach we felt important and grown-up. We would soon be heading to high school, which meant public school, which was both exciting and scary. Exciting because there'd be no more daily prayers; no more Orthodox rabbis who called their Cross pen *crose* so as not to vocalize a Christian symbol; no more school uniforms; no more compulsory recitations of *birkat hamazon*, the grace after meals prayer, with the principal's voice floating over the PA system as we ate our sandwiches and fruit roll-ups. Soon there would be guidance counselors and free periods called "spares," and tennis courts and a running track and teenagers everywhere, some with mustaches, and an outdoor smoking area called *the pit*, and hardcover yearbooks, and a drama studio and a woodworking shop, and students who drove to school. That afternoon, lying on towels next to our teacher at Kits Beach felt like a safe buffer between the two worlds.

Now I again find myself frightened by the uncertainty facing me: what if they don't capture all the cancerous cells? And even if they do, how do I protect myself from another growth in the future? While I've hardly suntanned since that day in seventh grade, I've just spent a year in Israel, one of the sunniest places on earth—and I plan to return. I feel helpless and alone. While all of us were in the same boat when it came to transitioning out of our little Jewish day school cocoon into the large public high school, now it's only me, among any of my friends, family or acquaintances, who's had a melanoma diagnosis.

"Just don't lie directly out in the sun, and you should be fine. Wear sunscreen. Just common sense stuff, really."

I think back to sitting on the sprawling lawn on my kibbutz in the northern Negev desert, where I spent many weekends, staring up at the tips of the palm trees almost spearing the April sun. I think about the afternoon I spent with two friends from the kibbutz, soldier boys, who took me on the back of a dirt bike to the surrounding desert, where we lazed around making sweet Turkish coffee in a *finjan* over a small camping stove while we grazed on sunflower seeds and ate chunks of Elite chocolate under the May Middle Eastern sun. I think about running through the field on that kindergarten field trip, the June Winnipeg sun hot on my back as my dad scooped me up for a weekend away at his friends' cottage. I think back to my summers at camp in Manitoba, where my friends and I would play rounds of Hearts on the beach under the July Manitoba sun. I think about standing on an overturned inflatable dingy near the shore of Lake Winnipeg, at my dad's cottage, the waning August sun illuminating my new self-guided sport, as I tried not to fall off but was delighted when I did.

Three years later, the "wear sunscreen" urban-legend graduation speech is published in the *Chicago Tribune* and becomes a staple of pop culture, and I will feel both seen and not seen. Seen because sunscreen is an essential part of my daily life. Not seen because "wear sunscreen" is all too often said lightly, in jest. And while sun safety will gradually become a commonsense matter, I will forever flinch when friends talk about wanting to "get some color" or when my stepmom, trying to compliment me, says "you look tanned!" and I have to remind her that UV rays are my kryptonite.

For the next twenty years, until a friend of mine a decade my senior gets a mole removed on her foot, which turns out to be a melanoma (I bring her containers of Häagen-Dazs as she recovers from surgery), I'll remain the only person I know who's been struck. I will stand out. But not for the reasons I want.

A week after my appointment with the surgeon, I walk from my apartment to Sherbrooke Street. I am sheltering my right arm with my left hand, fearful that another few minutes of sun exposure might accelerate the cancer. I board a city bus going westward. It's midday and the bus is mostly empty. I watch the buildings along Sherbrooke speed past me. The plaza where the Montreal band Me Mom and Morgentaler had played at frosh week three years ago, when I was a freshman, and first heard of Ska music. The Bronfman commerce building where my boyfriend, midway through second year, broke up with me after borrowing my McGill library card to take out books he couldn't get at his own university library across the street. The Musée des beaux-arts. And now, ten minutes later, we've arrived at the Jewish General Hospital.

I recall hearing about "The Jewish," as the hospital is known, when I was a teenager. My dad had trained there when he was in medical school, while my mom worked as an occupational therapist's assistant to support them. I'd been excited to hear that there was a hospital known as "The Jewish," but now I don't feel excited at all.

I pull the cord overhead and the bus driver stops to let me off. In the dim hospital room, I lie on my back as a doctor administers a local anesthetic. My plastic surgeon, I've heard, is known for his whistling skills.

"Can you whistle something to calm me down and cheer me up?" I laugh nervously.

"Hmm… how's this?"

He offers up a baroque-sounding tune from his airways as he aims a bright light onto my forearm. My arm has become a stage where the theatrical action—scalpel, flesh, needle, thread —is unfurling. He leans down toward me as I look away. Soon I feel bits of painless, dull pressure in the places where I know he is slicing into me before scooping out the deadly cells and stitching me up.

"Change your bandages twice a day. Take these for the pain." The nurse places a slip of paper with a prescription in my hand, pats my shoulder, and smiles.

This time I take a taxi home, rather than the bus. A few hours later, I'm back in my apartment with my forearm wrapped in thick white bandages and a bottle of painkillers on my desk.

That evening I walk a few blocks down Milton Street to the Leacock Building on campus. I am wearing my favorite denim cutoffs and a McGill T-shirt, enjoying the warm late-summer evening air without the glare of the sun. My arm is still wrapped in the same bandages; I can see bits of blood through the layers, and I've stashed the painkillers in my backpack just in case. The anesthetic is starting to wear off and I'm starting to feel a dull throbbing. But Michael Ondaatje is scheduled to read from his new book and I don't want to miss it. My stepmom had written to me while I was in Israel that she had gone to hear him read in Vancouver. "It was a religious experience," she wrote, a metaphor I lingered on, as I was spending the year in the epicenter of multiple world faiths.

I enter the lecture hall and look around for people I know. I don't see anyone. I take a seat near the back and stare straight ahead, at the stage. Ondaatje's voice soon fills the room. It's not quite a religious experience—I'm too anchored to the pain in my arm and the shock of the last few weeks' events to be totally transformed. And the content of *The English Patient* cuts perhaps too close to the bone, being about a burn victim, wrapped in bandages, and recovering in a wartime hospital. But being there in that lecture hall, surrounded by other students and faculty, alone and anonymous while also experiencing a sense of community, reminds me that life can return to normal. It's all a welcome distraction from the realization that I have been struck with cancer, even if the cancerous cells were *minimally invasive,* 0.6 mm, and even if all I'm supposed to do now is wear sunscreen.

Not long after, I'm flipping through my Israel year photos. One catches my eye. I am standing at the Jerusalem bus station. Above me is the sign for the bus to Be'er Sheva, where I'll head before catching the connecting bus to the kibbutz. My green backpack is slung over my shoulders and I'm wearing a green T-shirt with white circles and denim cutoffs. On my wrist is a painted wooden bracelet. I am holding some books. I probably had homework that weekend to complete between my work branch duties and the Friday night disco and visiting with my kibbutz family. And then, peering closely at the lower half of the photo, I see it: my lethal mole. The one that is now in some tissue repository in Vancouver, with its nearby cells in a hospital lab in Montreal, awaiting further testing. In its place, on my arm now, is a fat two-and-a-half-inch-long scar—resembling a stretched-out wristwatch—keeping time as I wait.

CHAPTER 6

Cabins

1981

"Do you have enough outfits for Shabbat?" my mom asks. It's my first summer at the Hebrew camp I've been waiting to be old enough to go to. She is glancing back and forth between the camp-issued packing list and the clothes piled next to the ironing board ready to have name labels affixed: twenty-one pairs of athletic socks, twenty-one pairs of underwear, six pairs of shorts, twelve T-shirts including my iron-on Saturday Night Fever shirt, three sweaters, two pairs of jeans, my Adidas track suit, matching wristbands, and my translucent blue plastic visor.

She sighs. "Go to your closet and pick out another nice dress. It's summer, so no need to bother with nylons."

Now it is my turn to sigh. But with relief. I am glad to leave the pantyhose—they always bunch and twist—at home. Plus, if they get a run, I'm supposed to ask my mom for clear nail polish to paint on right away, before the run gets worse, and I don't think I'll be able to find any at camp.

I reach up to the clothes hanging in my closet and notice the fancy outfit I most love: the purple satin skirt and matching blouse that comes with a black bow tie. I last wore that outfit to an evening out at the local dinner theater in South Winnipeg, with my mom and stepdad and some older relatives. My great-aunt, Helene Winston, was in the play. My parents always refer to her by her first and last name, because she's a bit famous. I know her mostly from TV. She plays the Jewish mother in the

© The Author(s) 2021
M. Sucharov, *Borders and Belonging: A Memoir*,
https://doi.org/10.1007/978-3-030-53732-6_6

show *The King of Kensington*. That night, at the dinner theater, I was one of the only kids among a sea of adults. I felt grown-up, sipping a Shirley Temple at a little round table facing the stage, just like in the movies.

My mom's voice jolts me back to the task at hand. "And make sure to pack your fancy sandals!"

It will probably be too hot at camp for that purple satin outfit. So I settle on a lightweight tan sundress. I rummage in the bottom of my closet and grab my sandals.

My dress and shoes in place, and with my mind on John Travolta and *Superman II* and the Quench drink crystals that my friends and I like to eat right out of the package, all that is left to do is count down the hours until I get to be away from all the carpets and the red spots on the stairs and away from me being *a riot* and *a scream* and away from everyone being jealous of me for things I don't actually want to have, and away from the *separating*.

At camp, my guts never swirl and flames never lick my insides. The only time I notice my guts is when I'm swirling them on purpose, while belting out my team songs so I can impress the Maccabiah and Yom Sport, Sports Day, and Televizia program judges with my *ru'ach*, my spirit.

When I sing and act in plays with the scripts written out in Hebrew and printed on Gestetner sheets, and when I put on the goofy costumes my counselors have picked out for the skits, and when I go all kooky to rack up *ru'ach* points for my Maccabiah team, keeping nearby the good luck charm that my dad has sent me for the competition—pink shoelaces stamped with colorful hearts—the counselors tell me I'm a *kochav*, a star.

The ghost stories, about a man named Jonathan Krepsie who the counselors tell us roams through the surrounding forest every night, don't actually scare me. At camp, the *ru'ach* carries me far away from actual scary things like Dimitri and his blood spots on our stairs, and away from scary Disney movies with amputated fingers and my dad's melty painting.

Camp means my embossed camp visor and my jean shorts and tank tops and bug juice and hot chocolate and pancakes with Beehive corn syrup in thick yellow bottles that have ridges that you squeeze and Hebrew songs and Hebrew-English puns and macramé bracelets that we try to keep on all year until they are hanging by a thread and we have to make new ones, and the Yom Sport tug-of-war where my palms chafe from grabbing the thick rope but I don't care because I'm cheering and yelling and we are about to win.

In my first letter home, I write "Dear Mom, here I am at camp, following in Daddy's footsteps." I try out my best cursive and I feel a sense of family history and I'm even starting to feel the *nostalgia* that the counselors try to get us to feel about the past at camp even though we're still only kids. I try to learn some of the old cabin songs, from years before I arrived, so I can participate in the *nostalgia*. Before I came to camp this summer, my dad taught me the song they used to sing about him, using his nickname:

Soochie gar b'veit hakiseh
lifamim mevaker et ha-machaneh

Soochie lives in the bathroom;
Sometimes he visits the camp.

When I've finished writing my letter about my counselors' names and the soccer baseball and the rock painting and the food—I like the cereal and hot chocolate and pancakes and cheese pie, but I don't much like the beef with green peppers—I slip the small piece of decorated stationery into the pre-addressed stamped envelope my mom sent with me. Tomorrow, during rest period after lunch, I will write a letter to my dad.

Camp means just me and three other friends from the neighborhood: Leah, Anna, and Jill, plus our two counselors. We are a little family that gets to live all together for three weeks in a white wooden cabin with green trim and a dark wooden floor instead of carpets, floors that we mop for Shabbat with Pine Sol before we put on our fancy dresses and sandals and gather around the flagpole to sing Hatikvah and then go to sit under the umbrella structure to recite kabbalat Shabbat prayers.

Leah and I have our own secret, though.

A few months before camp, Leah came over to my house for a sleep-over. First we played two rounds of Mastermind, and then we watched *The Love Boat* while eating from big bowls filled with maple-walnut ice cream. On the show, Doc and a pretty woman with long hair were drinking something they kept calling nightcaps.

Then it was bedtime. Leah arranged her sleeping bag on the brown carpet next to my bed. "You can borrow my flashlight to read," I said. I had a few more pages of *The Great Brain Returns* to get through.

After a few minutes, I turned to face her. "Hey," I whispered. I grabbed an extra nightie from my drawer. It was long and green, with a faded picture of Holly Hobbie on the front, and the fabric was starting to pill from wear. "If you roll a nightie tightly like this and place it right here, it feels good." I showed her how to scrunch the garment and place it between her legs. I instructed her to squeeze all her muscles and then relax.

She tried it. I heard her giggle, which made me giggle. It was good that the light was off, because she probably would have seen me blush and then I'd be blushing even more. Eventually, we fell asleep.

The next morning, I woke up first and went to the kitchen. Soon Leah joined me and I poured her a bowl of Rice Krispies.

"Wanna play Crazy Eights?" I asked.

"Sure."

We moved to the living room and sat cross-legged on the brown carpet. We were halfway through a round when my stepdad walked in. Leah looked at him and back at me. Then she rose from her spot on the floor, approached Ron, and stood on her tiptoes to whisper something in his ear. I quickly looked away.

When he'd gone into the kitchen, I glared at her. "What did you tell him?"

Her eyes flashed. "I told him about what you showed me last night." She raised her chin in defiance.

I lowered my gaze and we finished our game in silence.

What I had shown her was private, but it wasn't wrong—so it shouldn't have been a secret—or *was* it wrong? She had *told on me*, after all. And you tell on people when they do something wrong. So maybe it *was* wrong. I was confused. Anyway, Ron never mentioned it to me directly, and soon enough, I didn't think much of it.

But not long after, I was reading over the medical form for camp. There were questions about vaccinations and bedwetting and sleep-walking. I froze when I reached this question: "Does your child menstruate?" Menstruate. *Menstruate.* That word was familiar. I quickly folded up the form as I felt my cheeks burn. *Menstruate* was what we weren't supposed to do in the dark, in our room, even though it felt good. I hoped my mom wouldn't notice that question. And if she did, I prayed that she wouldn't ask me about it. She already tried to talk to me about too many things. Sometimes she'd perch on the edge of my bed.

"Is there anything you want to tell me?" she'd ask.

"No thanks, I'm fine," I'd say, turning away and burrowing into my book.

Her questions made my stomach swirl. Was there something I was *supposed* to tell her? Something that I was hiding? Maybe this *menstruation* is what she meant.

On Yom Sport, I'm picked to run the evening races. I unlace my navy Nikes with the white stripe, remove my athletic socks, and run barefoot, because I've heard that's what serious runners do. I'm picked to represent my team and Leah is picked to represent hers.

"Good luck," she says, and smirks.

I look around at the rows of campers sitting and watching, and I make eye contact with my counselors, before crouching down low. When the whistle blows, I run as fast as I can toward the outhouses, before seeing Leah pass me in the next lane.

"Nice try," she says.

I manage a half-smile and wipe my brow with my terry cloth wristband.

On Sadie Hawkins Day, Leah and I have a silent agreement. We will each chase different boys. I decide to chase after Charlie, the thirteen-year-old with the nice shoulders and no shirt and red rugby shorts, who leads me in figure eights around the boys' cabins and then the outhouses and then down the center field near the flagpole, until I finally feel the tips of my fingers graze his smooth back.

Leah picks Paul, Charlie's cabinmate, and catches him near the *marp*, the infirmary. After the race, we all make our way to the wedding chuppah set up for couples in the *ulam*, the program hall. Charlie presents me with a tiny ring with a green stone and the director declares us married. I treasure that little ring. Then we all dance our hearts out to the Doobie Brothers and the Hollies and the Kinks, pausing at 9:30, when the Manitoba sun sets, to sit in a circle and recite havdalah, the ceremony marking the end of the Sabbath, as our eyes are mesmerized by the flame on the braided candle. "A good week" we sing, in Hebrew, English, French, Yiddish, and Russian, before getting up and hoping we get asked by the person we most want to dance with for "Stairway to Heaven."

Leah and I are always on opposing teams. Our first year at camp, her Maccabiah team, named *bidur* (entertainment), beats my team, *ochel* (food). Same with the second year: *dat* (religion), against *briut* (health). By third year and fourth year, I have a small winning streak. But I can't gloat because Leah isn't at camp those years. Her parents take her on a family vacation to Toronto instead.

A couple of weeks into camp, a throng of us are washing up at the outdoor sinks. The sinks smell of rust and the area is hemmed in by screens to protect us from the Manitoba mosquitos. Tonight, the screens are lined with the tiny feet of dozens of fish flies, a kind of burrowing mayfly that is common in these parts of Manitoba. *Zvuvei dag*, we call them, in camp-style Hebrew, where we take the word for fish and the word for housefly and imitate the nickname in direct translation. It sounds better, at least, then when we call cottage cheese *gvinat tzrif* (cabin cheese).

We are fascinated by the fish flies, but we hate when their short lives are over and hundreds of their corpses crunch underfoot as we walk to the lake, the stench of rotting exoskeletons floating upwards. But we love capturing them alive on the backs of our hands and gently pinching their wings and watching them squirm. We aren't trying to be cruel, but like everything else at camp—the lake, the highway, the prairie sky, and even the trees the counselors cut down if they need to create a forest set for one of the evening programs, these fish flies, we believe, belong to us. Our favorite kind are the tiny green ones. Soon they will turn tan, and then brown, and then they will die. But while they are green, they are small and fresh and sweet and all ours.

I finish washing my face, enjoying the feel of the hot water flowing from the tall faucet, and replace my bar of soap in its pink plastic soap dish. I turn to Harry. He's a tall, jovial, zany counselor, and we all admire him.

Harry meets my smile.

"Camp really suits you," he says. "You know, you're a star."

"I am?" My eyes widen as I soak in the praise.

"You absolutely are. But having that kind of talent can be a burden." He pauses and looks down. "Of course, I can totally relate."

I'm not sure which talent he means, exactly, but I figure it's my penchant for singing my heart out or reciting my lines clearly in plays or for always making an effort to speak Hebrew.

"How is it a pain?" I ask.

He explains in a mix of Hebrew and English that when he was younger, his parents and their friends would ask him to sing songs and recite dramatic monologues on command. "I felt like a performing seal. I bet you feel that way too sometimes," he says.

"Yeah, I guess I do," I say, putting my soap dish back in my toiletries case.

A performing seal. I picture a seal bouncing a beach ball on its nose. But the truth is that I have never minded being a *performing seal.* I eagerly recite my French poems—rehearsing them for the citywide competition in elementary school—to whoever is willing to hear them. I love sitting at the piano, belting out the chords to the title song from the *Fame!* album and to "Let's Get Physical" by Olivia Newton John. Except for the time I got so carried away while playing that I slid right off the piano bench—my mom had shined it with Pledge that afternoon and it was slippery—and hit my head on the window ledge. I touched my hair and it felt warm and sticky and I had to go to the hospital for stitches.

I like impressing the grown-ups when I'm my mom's partner for Password, giving single-word clues to her across our family friends' living room at dinner parties. I like speaking up around adults. I like being asked to perform. I like *participating*, but sometimes that makes grown-ups annoyed, like when my older relatives squint their eyes and push their eyebrows down into angry angles when I tell them that their jokes about *goys* and *Polaks* are wrong. It is wrong to be *prejudiced* and to make jokes about people who are different from you. I tell them that too. But they scowl and turn away.

And sometimes it gets me into trouble, the sort of trouble that I'm kind of proud of and also a bit embarrassed by, like the time at camp when I was nine, and I snuck into the oldest boys' cabin when no one was there so I could borrow their counselor's jeans and varsity basketball jacket. For the costume ball that night, I was planning to dress up as him. When the counselor saw me wearing his clothes, he wasn't impressed and delighted, as I'd hoped he would be. "Dammit Mira! I was looking for those jeans all afternoon!" he said.

Sometimes it's the kind of trouble that makes my cheeks burn, like the time I was jumping on the trampoline in the backyard of my grandparents' friends, down the street from their house in Vancouver. My stomach was swirling in the good way and my nose was filled with the scent of lilac and azaleas.

That afternoon, as I looked toward the open window into the sunken family room where the teenage son and daughter kept their Kiss records, and as I felt the sun on my face, I listened to the parents having an argument. "That sucks!" I heard the wife yell to her husband as she came into the yard.

Sensing an opening, I blurted out, "Do you mean 'that sucks' like *sucking on a lollipop?*" Continuing to jump, I looked toward her expectantly. But the wife returned my attempt at a joke with a sharp glare.

"Mind your own business, Mira! Haven't your parents taught you that it's rude to eavesdrop?"

I jumped a little slower now, looking down at the orange tarp and blue springs, my face hot with embarrassment. I guess I did know that it was rude to eavesdrop. But I liked participating. And the best way to participate, I had learned, was first to listen to grown-up conversations around me. I guess that was a type of eavesdropping.

This conversation with Harry at the sinks at camp as we're washing up is the first time a grown-up has commiserated with me over anything. And it's the first time I've felt the rush that a shot of external affirmation, from an adult who is older than my cousins and my babysitters, but younger than my parents and teachers, gives me. That rush will eventually become addictive.

The next summer at camp, I moonlight as our cabin DJ every night at bedtime, playing the cassettes I've brought with me: *Grease*, *Fiddler on the Roof*, *Simon and Garfunkel's Greatest Hits*, and a concert album by Chai, Winnipeg's Jewish youth song and dance troupe. I've brought my portable Toshiba boom box from home, which I've secured to my metal cot with a red bike lock. We play tapes but never flick the lever of the radio. We don't want to hear CJOB newscasters talking about the sports scores or relaying traffic reports; we don't want to hear their metallic voices announcing beefs and bouquets; we don't want to hear jingles for car washes and pizza. We don't want anything to breach the walls of our summer camp cocoon. Plus, those newscasts are in English.

One day Ryan, a friend from another cabin who is a year younger than us, comes to visit our bunk during rest period, after lunch. Ryan is smart and mature for his age and has a ready smile. *Peulat gimmel b'eser dakot!* The loudspeaker interrupts our conversation. The third activity period is starting in ten minutes. I put down my *Archie Digest* and get up off my bed. The next period is sports. We're headed to the *ulam* to play floor hockey: my favorite. I figure I should take off my jeans and slip on my shorts. I start to undress. As my underwear comes into view, my cabinmates gesticulate wildly in my direction before looking at Ryan.

I feel my cheeks burn and then the sting of tears, as I rush to cover up. "I didn't realize," I say, mumbling. Ryan is blushing too.

It was not the first time I had shown a boy my underwear. When I was six, I was at the house of family friends whose two older sons had been tasked with watching me after school every day until my mom finished her courses at the local community college. First, the three of us would take the bus down Grant Avenue from our Jewish day school to their house. Normally, we would sit in their carpeted basement watching *The Match Game* and *Gilligan's Island*, with a poster of Muhammad Ali staring down at us. *Fly Like a Butterfly, Sting Like a Bee.*

One afternoon, the eleven-year-old brother turned to me. "Wanna go upstairs?" he asked. I followed him up the two flights of stairs, to his mother's room. She'd be out for at least another hour. He sat on the unmade bed and motioned for me to follow. "Show me your private parts," he said, as he leaned over me. Slowly, I undid the waist-tie of my red cable-knit sweater, and then carefully opened each brown leather button. I undid the snap of my jeans, pulled down the zipper, and slid my pants down. My cheeks burned with shame, humiliation, curiosity, and fear.

By the next day I felt only sadness, guilt, and stomach swirling. My dad rang the doorbell to pick me up at my mom's house for our regular visit.

"Hi Daddy," I said. Then I crumpled.

Clutching my favorite book—*Danny, the Champion of the World*—I struggled to get the words out through my tears, as I recounted to my parents what had happened in the bed of that family friend. My parents looked at me intently, an expression of concern etched into their faces, before hugging me as I continued to cry.

I no longer went back to that house after school. Instead, each day, I packed up my red knapsack and walked to an after-school home daycare my mom had found near my school, where the caregiver poured us glasses of milk from bags she retrieved from the freezer, which meant that bits of ice were always floating in the milk, and I clenched my teeth as I drank it down. I watched too much TV there, and I was bored and lonely and felt too old.

During the post-lunch singalong at camp most days, Yossi, a counselor-in-training who I have a crush on, motions to me to sit on his lap. I do. My stomach flips and flops, but this swirling is one I love. *Hey, Hey Yona/Hey Yona Pa'amona* we sing in Hebrew, as we go through each verse with heightened enthusiasm, each year of camp giving us a little more understanding of what the lyrics, which are simple wordplay on gender roles and carnality, actually mean. When we get to the final line, which is full of sexual innuendo, we scream it out. I tap Yossi's knees through his gray sweatpants as I chant.

When I return from camp, I tell my parents about Yossi. "He even let me sit on his lap during after-lunch singing! We all thought he was cute. He's a total hunk."

My mom, sitting in the passenger seat of my stepdad's Buick, looks over at him and then into the backseat, at me. "Mira, that's not appropriate. You shouldn't sit on male counselors' laps. It's not right."

I look down at my own lap. I think to myself how badly I want to sit on Yossi's lap again next year. I wonder whether sitting on his lap is wrong. I let out a long sigh and decide not to tell them about the good-night kisses we sometimes got from our favorite counselors. And I don't mention the dirty words the director taught us, words like *coitus inter-ruptus*. We're not allowed to speak English at our Hebrew-only camp, at least not officially, but Latin is okay.

"What does it mean?" we asked the director, our eyes wide. Her presence in our cabin at bedtime felt like a special occasion. Like the prime minister paying us an official visit.

"One day you'll know." She laughed. "Or maybe you won't have to know!" We looked at one another, puzzled. Then we broke the awkwardness by laughing and repeating the phrase, *coitus interruptus,* over and over, until we fell asleep.

We are sitting on the floor in the *ulam* on Friday night, in messy rows, counselors interspersed with campers. Our bellies are full from chicken soup and challah and the grape juice we are served in tiny cups. The song leader is flipping transparencies onto the overhead projector. My eyes adjust to the Hebrew letters as the hall fills with the sweet sound of dozens of young voices singing about the beauty of Sharm a Sheikh, the Red Sea desert town.

I catch on quickly and join in, following along a couple of words behind during the verses, but by the time the chorus has repeated a second and then third time I'm belting it out. I'm no longer at the Charter House restaurant before my weekly appointment with Dr. James, feeling the pinballs ricocheting off the inside of my chest. I am here, at camp, feeling the varnished wood beneath me, as I sit cross-legged, my knees touching Leah's to my right and Jenny's to my left, singing the most beautiful song I've ever heard, in what will soon become my favorite language on earth.

A decade later, I will be at the Hebrew University of Jerusalem studying on the overseas program. Semester break approaches and someone suggests a trip to the Sinai. "We can go to Dahab," my friend says, "but if we have the time we should really try to get to Sharm. The snorkeling is awesome there."

I'll flash back to the program hall at camp where we sang the most beautiful song about Sharm A Sheikh that was mostly just words and melody to me when I was nine. But of course I will now know it is actually a place in another country that Israel had conquered in the 1967 War, and held until Israel and Egypt signed a peace treaty in 1979, after which Israel eventually withdrew from the Sinai Peninsula. The song, I will learn, was a song of Israeli military victory, and was written by Ran Eliran and Amos Ettinger to comfort and entertain the IDF troops as they fought the Egyptians in the 1967 war. And my memories of singing my favorite song at camp will be tempered as I realize there are geopolitics involved. And while we opt for Cairo and Luxor instead as our travel destination on that semester break, where we snap photos of the Egyptian soldiers guarding the Suez Canal and eat kushari from street stands and ride camels and donkeys at the foot of the pyramids and ride an overnight bus to Luxor and visit the inspiration for Shelley's "Ozymandias" poem that we studied in high school, and where a man rubs his hands up and down me on a crowded Cairo bus and we have to push away the felucca drivers who try to grope us while we are falling asleep on the Nile and where shopkeepers selling scarabs and cartouches tell us approvingly that Jews are shrewd and clever, before we rebuke them and they end up apologizing, I will eventually make it to Sharm a couple of years later, and then again five years after that.

My husband and I will be living in Jerusalem for nine months when we decide to travel to Sinai, to Sharm-al-Sheikh, to spend New Year's Eve. On December 31, 1999, we play cards and eat Cadbury's Fruit and Nut chocolate bars with other tourists under makeshift tents on the beach, hoping the world doesn't end as the clock switches to Jan. 1, 2000. I can't blame the Israelis for still singing longingly of a place that is no longer theirs: the desert abutting the sea, the coral reefs populated by an explosion of color as striped and mottled fish seek food and shelter, is stunning to behold. I will push away my political thoughts about the

Arab–Israeli conflict for a few days at least, so my husband and I, who are still newlyweds, can ring in the new millennium.

And when we have to *separate* at the end of each summer at camp, singing "*eneini rotzeh lashuv*, I don't want to return (to the city)," standing in a long semicircle, with our arms around each other in the *chadar ochel* after a pancake breakfast the final morning as we wait for the buses to spirit us back to our parents and teachers and cars and radios and television and errands and the news, we know it's only eleven months until camp starts again. That kind of *separation* is sad, but it's the good kind of sad. We revel in the tears of *that* separation because those tears mean we're growing up. We now harbor longing not only for our houses and our parents and our school and our teachers and the long sidewalks and our evening bike rides on the flat prairie streets, but also for each other, and for summer camp.

CHAPTER 7

Peace, Love, and Conflict

1993

"Are you coming over to Justin's this afternoon?" It's my friend Oren on the phone. I'm in my apartment and he's in his. "We're going to watch the Israeli-Palestinian peace ceremony. Maybe Yasser Arafat will even shave for it." He laughs at his own joke.

Justin is one of the few friends in our social circle at McGill who owns a TV. It's generally not considered cool. For entertainment we go to movies at the repertory cinema on St. Catherine, taping the monthly schedule to our refrigerators. For news, we subscribe to *The New York Times*, which we pick up every day from the student union building.

The last time we all watched TV together was in our freshman year, when we gathered every night in early second semester in the common room of McConnell Hall to watch the Gulf War unfold in real time. That year, in January 1991, we watched Iraqi Scud missiles raining down on Tel Aviv while Palestinians cheered. This year, in September 1993, we will witness Israelis and Palestinians finally making peace.

At Justin's, I take my place on one of the kitchen chairs arranged in a semi-circle in the living room. We face the screen as President Bill Clinton prods Yitzhak Rabin toward Arafat, for what will become the famous handshake between the two men. We cheer and toast to what seems like a new era. We are proud progressive Zionists, looking forward to a new chapter of peace to unfold in the country we love almost as much as our own, or perhaps even more.

© The Author(s) 2021
M. Sucharov, *Borders and Belonging: A Memoir*,
https://doi.org/10.1007/978-3-030-53732-6_7

From media reports we learn that Rabin used a Pilot-brand pen to sign the historic document. "Hilarious," I say to my friend Adam. "Only a sabra like Rabin would use a drugstore pen to sign the Declaration of Principles." I can't wait to get back to Israel. After we graduate, Adam and I plan to room together, along with another friend from McGill, in an apartment in Tel Aviv.

The next day, reading the coverage of the peace deal in the *Globe and Mail*, I clip the letters of mutual recognition that Rabin and Arafat have written each other. I tack them to my bedroom wall, just above my desk. It's early in the school year, and I figure we'll have lots to talk about in our Arab-Jewish dialogue group. But I'm not prepared for what awaits.

"We won't sit and dialogue anymore," the leader of the group says the next time we meet in the Arts building on campus. "Dialogue means normalizing the agreement, legitimizing it. We don't want to give our support to it. It's a real defeat for the Palestinians, as I'm sure you know."

Defeat? It seems like a victory to me. The PLO has managed to tame Israel's adventurist impulses, even with their meager power. The Palestinians stand to gain a long-denied state. But still, I listen. He has seemed nice enough since we first met, and the fact that he was interested in engaging in dialogue with us in the first place says something. I'm willing to grant that he might be right. But my natural optimism persists.

Another member joins in. "Did you see what Edward Said said about the deal? He called it a Palestinian Versailles."

I picture Rabin and Arafat shaking hands. I hear Rabin's speech, drawing from Ecclesiastes, echo in my head: "there is a time for everything." If Rabin—the warrior—says there is a time for peace, shouldn't we believe him? Cynicism has no place here, I think. It's Canada. It's McGill. It's Montreal: the city of jazz, poetry, the Habs and smoked meat. Can't we just be happy?.

But the Arab student group remains steadfast. I leave the seminar room, my shoulders hunched, and walk down the steps toward the Milton gates, letting out a long sigh. This will be the last time we meet as a group, and this will be my first time experiencing first-hand what will later become more widely known as "anti-normalization." This is the belief that dialogue for its own sake, meaning sitting and talking without actively pledging to overturn the structures of oppression and inequity first, is a way of shoring up the status quo, rather than resisting it. We all claimed to oppose the occupation of the West Bank and Gaza. But our differing views of what would soon become known as the Oslo agreement was enough to sever the connection we had made.

Years later, I will publish an op-ed in the *Globe and Mail*, spurred by the death of Shimon Peres. The "constructive ambiguity of the Oslo Agreement—the idea that the toughest topics: settlements, refugees and final borders—would be deferred to later rounds of negotiations arguably enabled the agreement to get signed," I will write, adding, "But Mr. Peres would have also known that the vague deferrals in the Oslo Agreement also carried the seeds of its destruction. Two decades later, peace between Israelis and Palestinians remains elusive."

Maybe the Arab students who stepped away from our dialogue group because they couldn't countenance the Oslo Agreement—which most everyone, no matter what they thought of it at the time, will eventually agree is "dead" with little to show for it—were right after all. To those of us who'd cherished it as we did, supporters of Israel and supporters of peace, maybe that agreement was a false prize, like the bookmark my teacher gave me in third grade.

My third-grade teacher, a stocky Israeli who sported a wide smile and favored brown dress pants, brown leather slip-on dress shoes, and beige short-sleeve V-neck collared shirts, called me to his desk one morning. "If you can get through *one day* without being sent out of the room," he said with a twinkle in his eye, "this bookmark will be yours."

Usually, I was sent out of the room at least once a day. That year, I craved attention. My parents had an explanation for my antics: my mom had just gotten remarried, and I was reliving the anxiety of the divorce. On the days I got sent out, I would curl up on the threadbare orange carpet in the vestibule between our classroom trailer and the main school, willing myself to sleep in a paltry act of civil disobedience that never worked.

My teacher held up the bookmark for me to examine. The cardboard strip was encased in plastic and woven with gray thread along the edges. On one side were Israeli coins; on the other Israeli postage stamps. I was transfixed.

Until 10:30 a.m., I had managed to stay quiet and attentive. But then, in a lesson on Hebrew grammar, I sensed an opening. "Masculine and feminine endings are so funny! Words don't have private parts!" I yelled. I burst out laughing and looked around. My laughter had become contagious and soon the classroom was a cacophony of giggles and repetitions of the phrase *private parts*.

The teacher turned from the blackboard to face me. "Mira, *tze'i me-ha-kita*. Leave the classroom." My head down, I rose from my seat and walked the ten feet toward the door, taking my regular spot on the orange carpet.

At the end of the afternoon, my teacher called me up to his desk. "You did get sent out of the room today," he said carefully in Hebrew, the corners of his mouth curling upwards to form the beginning of a smile. "But I know you tried."

He handed me the bookmark, and I took the unearned prize in my hand, my face burning with both pride and shame.

I felt embarrassed by that small injustice, even though it ended in my favor. And yet I treasured that prize for years afterward. It was like my own fluffy pita and falafel—the cuisine that has become contested in the Middle East, with Israelis claiming it as theirs and Palestinians saying it's been appropriated. That bookmark was my personal Zionism, my kibbutz, my worn cotton army T-shirt, my potato fields, my Oslo, my Fallujah.

"*Of course* Zionism is problematic." Ben is a Jewish classmate in one of my Middle East Studies seminars, and we've become close friends. "All types of nationalism are." We're walking through campus together and I'm having trouble getting my head around his take on Israeli ideology.

As a Middle East Studies major, I've already taken all the Middle East politics courses available to undergrads. So my program advisor has let me enroll in two PhD-level courses. I'm surrounded by graduate students who both inspire me and make me nervous. Already I've used the word "normative" in the wrong way in an essay. "How is the theory normative?" my professor wrote in the margins. The truth is, I don't really know. I feel comfortable with Ben, though, who is struggling to figure out his own academic passions.

Ben and I are walking from the student union building toward Sherbrooke. "Look how much misery, violence, and war nationalism has brought to the world," Ben continues. "You can't honestly say that you think nationalism is a *good* thing."

"Well, I kinda think it's good. I mean it's better than religious fundamentalism, isn't it? I mean, everyone can work together to build a nation. I mean, a state." Now I'm confusing myself.

In my Labor Zionist circles, we used to say that nationalism was good. Jewish nationalism, that is. We saw our Zionism—progressive Zionism, we called it—as extending directly from social consciousness. At our summer camp, we expressed our Labor Zionism through secularism. Instead of reciting the *hamotzi* blessing before meals, we sang socialist worker songs. And Shabbat involved beach walks and songs rather than any of the traditional Shabbat prayers. That made it seem even more appealing. In pushing back on a lot of the religious orthodoxy that governed our communities growing up, we thought we were offering a cool, modern, enlightened alternative.

And not only did we think it was cool and modern, we thought it was fair. We believed we had to demand not only Jewish national rights but Palestinian national rights too. We called for a two-state solution. That way, the Palestinians could have a country too; they too could be in charge of their own fate. Zionism—Jewish nationalism—could easily exist alongside Palestinian nationalism. Or so we believed.

"Nationalism." He adopts a lilting tone. "Is basically a form of chauvinism."

Chauvinism. I had only ever heard the word in the gender sense; I never thought a woman could be a chauvinist. And I guess I never thought that Jews, as a group, could be either. I picture myself sprawled on the lawn of my kibbutz, propped up on one elbow, with a sign affixed to my back: *Jewish chauvinist pig.* I flinch.

"But Jewish nationalism is different," I say, my voice rising a bit now. "It's about Jews taking charge of our own destiny. It doesn't have to mean we think we're any better than anyone else. I certainly don't think that. All nations deserve a state. Besides," I add, "Jewish nationalism has come with a total physical rebirth. You know, 'Jewry of muscle'—the thing that Zionist philosopher Max Nordau talked about. We are now working the land and using our own bodies for it. How awesome is that?"

I've been taking a philosophy of Zionism course this semester and Max Nordau is one of my favorite philosophers, along with A.D. Gordon and anyone who talks about working the land. My kibbutz. My potatoes. My combine. Gitai. The fields at Fallujah.

"Jewry of Muscle?" Ben shoots back. "That sounds positively fascist!"

I'm perplexed. Ben is Jewish. And he's not religious. So isn't Zionism actually the right thing for him? Everyone needs some hook on which to hang their identity. Wouldn't Zionism be it? The truth is, as much as I love Israel and my personal version of Zionism, I want Ben's approval. I love our long phone chats and strolls around campus and late nights at dive bars and drinking red wine in his apartment while watching Jim

Jarmusch movies along with his roommate, another graduate student. They pay lots of attention to me and make me feel special.

But I also believe I have the power of Jewish history behind me, and a Labor Zionist youth movement here in Montreal where we gather for Shabbat dinners to eat challah and ratatouille and drink red wine from a box, and where we are certain that our version of Zionism is the nice kind, the progressive kind, the kind that pushes for good in the world. Plus, the Labor Zionism I studied and taught at camp was sexy and cool. Or at least those were my associations from the nights I spent in the camp library on an abandoned mattress, surrounded by the writings of Zionist thinkers and awash in desire for my summer crush, whose favorite Zionist thinker was Ber Borochov.

A few weeks after my debate with Ben, I'm at the meeting of the Middle East Studies journal, where I've joined the student-led editorial board. Across from me is an Arab graduate student named Jabir. He is lean and stylish, with a slight British-inflected accent. He speaks slowly and deliberately, his eyes glinting with the intimation of a private joke whenever he says something that is meant to be ironic. When I manage to catch his eye, my stomach flips. But this time, I don't want to curb the sensation.

"Who wants to edit the essay on Arab civil society?" the head editor asks. "We need two volunteers."

"I can take that one," I say. I'm looking at Jabir, half-hoping he doesn't notice my stare.

Jabir raises his hand. "And so can I."

As the meeting comes to a close, I linger, and so does Jabir. "Do you want to meet this weekend? To do the edits?"

My heart beating quickly, I make a show of flipping through my agenda book. "Yeah, that works."

We meet on Sunday in the Middle East Studies student offices on a rented floor in a new downtown office building. We talk about the essay we're editing and we talk about our backgrounds. "I know you're from Lebanon, but are you Palestinian?" I ask.

He gives me a puzzled look. "What you makes you think that?" His lips curl downward around the edges.

"I know there are a lot of Palestinians in Lebanon," I say. I go quiet for a moment. His reaction tells me that issues of ethnicity and status, especially in countries where citizenship and belonging are contested, are rawer than I'd realized.

After we've finished the editing, Jabir gets up and walks toward the kitchenette. "Coffee, tea, or me?" he asks. His eyes twinkle.

I have never drunk coffee and I'm too bashful to tell him which of the other two options I really want, so I say that tea would be great. He brings back a mug of peppermint tea, and as he hands it to me, my fingers graze his. I take a sip before placing it on the desk.

It's winter in Montreal, dry-skin season. As I frequently do, I reach for my lip balm: Body Shop strawberry flavored. As I dip my finger into the small tub and smear the waxy contents over my lips, I catch Jabir looking at me.

After a beat, I look away. "Thank you for the tea," I say, "you shouldn't have," and we both laugh.

A week later, we're sitting across from one another at a round wooden table in a downtown cafe. I glance at my watch and realize we've been here for almost three hours. We've been talking about our families and our courses and our career plans.

"I love Almodovar," I say. "I think his latest film is playing at the Cinémathèque this week."

"Let's go together," he says. "Are there Almodovar films in Israel?" He is teasing now, as he knows that in a few months I'm headed to Tel Aviv for the year, after I spend the summer in my hometown of Vancouver. "Or do they only show films by settler-colonial directors over there?"

"Spain has its own colonial history," I counter, matching his gaze. A few months earlier I was embarrassed after asking my roommate's Latino boyfriend why, given how far Central America was from Spain, they speak Spanish there. He looked at me like I was nuts, or simply ignorant, and I guess I was.

"Um, have you ever heard of colonialism?" my roommate had said, through a loud and warm laugh. But her message was clear.

Then and there, I vowed never again to let basic global and historical dynamics escape me, whether or not I'd studied them in my coursework.

"I said *settler*-colonialism, not ordinary colonialism," Jabir says, lingering on the "t" and "l" blend, as my chest tingles.

"Hey, we're about to close," the waitress says, handing us our check. Jabir grabs it.

"I have tea back at my apartment," I offer. "Many flavors." I smile.

"Many flavors?" he says, eyebrows rising. "How many?"

"You can come count for yourself."

On the way to my apartment, we stop at the *depanneur*, whose aisles I know intimately from the ice-cream sandwiches, mediocre red wine, and Sara Lee frozen chocolate cake I often buy for late-night study-cram sessions. Jabir spots a box of condoms and looks at me. I look away as he reaches for them. And then I reach toward the small of his back, running my hand along the leather belt through the loops at the back of his jeans, as he approaches the counter.

A month earlier, I had been sitting with Jabir and some other students in the cafe at the student union building. Sunlight was streaming in through the windows. A student association volunteer approached our table, holding a basket filled with colorful plastic wrappers. "Condoms?" she asked. "It's safe-sex awareness week. Help yourself; they're free!"

"None for me," Jabir deadpanned. "It's Ramadan." My tablemates burst out laughing. I had no idea what the laws about sex during Ramadan were, and so I just laughed along, nodding. But amidst the laughter, my mind was running to having safe sex—or any sex at all—with Jabir.

Soon, we arrive at my apartment. We enter the second-floor suite with its green painted wood floors and bay window overlooking Hutchison Street. It's one of my final nights here before I graduate. It's a little bittersweet, thinking about my undergrad years wrapping up, and many of the friends I've made going our separate ways. But I have at least another year in Israel to look forward to before grad school and real life begins. The streets of Tel Aviv, the possibility of an enriching internship, and my return to the Hebrew-speaking land I so love, are intoxicating. Still, this new connection with Jabir has overtaken my every sense and the idea of suddenly being apart just as we've come together unsettles me. I push those thoughts away.

"I can put on the kettle," I say. And suddenly our bodies are locked together on my double futon set low in a pine frame. Above us hang my *Rime of the Ancient Mariner* poster; some camp photos, and the letters of mutual recognition, printed on yellowing newsprint, that Yitzhak Rabin and Yasser Arafat had exchanged seven months earlier.

The next morning I am filled with euphoria laced with dread. Jabir is staying in Montreal. He will probably be traveling back to the Middle East too, to visit his family. While I'm in Tel Aviv in a few months, he and I will be pretty nearby to one another, as the crow flies. But geopolitically, we will be as far away as two people can be.

"Come visit me in Vancouver." I trace a circle on his shoulder with my finger.

"Maybe I will." He kisses me and pulls me toward him. Neither of us mentions Israel.

On the week of my birthday in June, my mom hands me an envelope. I recognize Jabir's delicate cursive from when we worked on the journal edits together. I tear it open to find a card with a Rene Magritte print: the one with a man wearing a trench coat and bowler hat, a Granny Smith apple suspended in midair, obscuring the man's face. On the left-hand side of the card, Jabir has written "Happy Birthday Mira & a million more to come" in English, followed by an Arabic phrase. Despite my two years of literary Arabic training, I can't decipher it. I'll ask him about it on the next phone call. On the righthand side of the card, he's written this:

Dearest Mira,

In this wretched existence of ours, few people indulge themselves in the experiences of the "other." The travails are myriad, but the pleasures of such an experience are necessarily elevating.

You have willfully forced me into one such experience upon whose pleasures I shall remain silent, not for lack of will but for the inefficacy of words.

After all, our "being-in-the-world" is always a "being-with-the other."

Confusedly yours,

J

I read the card over and over, memorizing the flourishes of his handwriting. I'm charmed by his attempt to couch his romantic passion in academic prose. We met, after all, while editing a student journal article anchored in political theory. And my heart skips a beat when I read the word "pleasures." But I also worry that his use of the phrase "one such experience" could mean that he is already thinking of our relationship in a finite sense, as a single experience that will later be dwarfed by many others in his life. Most of all, I desperately hope that the apparent confusion in his "Confusedly yours" doesn't lead him to walk away.

Two weeks later, I'm at the Vancouver airport, waiting by the baggage carousel for Jabir. I look toward the opening leading to the gates, my heart beating quickly. I had asked Jabir, a week earlier, how he was feeling about coming to visit. "Expectant," he said. I puzzled over that response, but decided to read it positively. Suddenly I see him, walking toward me. He's holding a single paperback book.

"You pack light," I say, and we embrace. He is dressed smartly, in light-blue jeans, loafers, and a stylish suede jacket. His eyes twinkle as they always do when he meets my gaze, and I smile. And then I take his hand and lead him to retrieve his suitcase.

The next day we drive to Whistler, listening to the Gypsy Kings on the way as I navigate the picturesque sea-to-sky highway in my parents' Ford Taurus. In our rented condo, we fall onto the bed in an embrace. But a minute later, Jabir rolls away and stumbles into the bathroom. I can hear him throwing up. My pulse quickens. I want to believe it's food poisoning or innocent nerves rather than revulsion at our cross-ethnic connection. His comment, in the card he wrote, about being confused, still haunts me.

Soon he is back, and he doesn't say anything about what just happened. Over the next two days, we make up for it. We stay inside more than we go outside. In the afternoons we eat Neapolitan ice cream and don't bother getting dressed. At night we dine on sushi in the Whistler village. On the final afternoon, we talk about whether we could, hypothetically, sustain a relationship.

"I think we can. There are no red flags that I see," I say. "We do have quite a connection." I look into his eyes and smile, and he takes my hand. We are walking together over a mound of dirt and stones, enjoying the summer air filtered by the mountain pines. Neither of us mentions the most obvious of the potential barriers: the mountain of cross-cultural politics and identity issues that we would have to scale were we to stay together into the future. I'd met Jabir's brother once, and he was cordial enough, but a derisive streak lurked. "The only place Jews and Arabs can ever get along is in the Gucci store," he had said over a meal that Jabir had cooked for the three of us. And while my two sets of parents welcomed him warmly into their homes, his parents still live in the Middle East. Who knows where or when I would meet them, and how they'd react to him dating a Jew who identifies as a Zionist: a progressive, liberal Zionist, but a Zionist, still. Yet I'm hopeful we can transcend all that. I need for us to, anyway. I dread having to forcefully extinguish my growing affection for him.

When Jabir returns to Montreal, I long for his smile, his laugh, his smooth skin, the skip in his step. We talk on the phone and exchange letters. But a few weeks into our time apart again, I receive another letter.

Dearest Mira

How are you? I am jobless, with this lingering summer stretching ahead.

I pause over his endearing use of English. *Jobless* rather than aimless.

Something happened this week that I have to tell you about. Yesterday, I got a call from Amir. He told me to meet him at the research offices downtown.

Amir is also a grad student, an Arab friend of Jabir's. I picture my afternoon with Jabir at that office all those weeks ago now. My lip balm. His coffee-tea-or-me invitation.

When I arrived, they sat me down. They asked me why I'm always spending time with minorities.

He mentions his friend who is a Coptic Christian. He mentions another Catholic friend. Then he mentions me and my stomach flips.

I felt cornered. I was angry. But then I realized that we are, indeed, in a great predicament. You are going to live in Israel for the year. Maybe longer. What would happen if someone in my family found a letter from you bearing an Israeli postage stamp?

My heart is racing.

It's simply not going to work between us. My feelings for you are great. Your smile. Your lined lips. And it hurts me to write these words. But the time has come to say goodbye.

I squeeze my eyes shut as my guts swirl. I go to my room, shut the door, and cry.

The next morning, I drive from my parents' house in Richmond, BC, to Denny's on Southwest Marine drive, in Vancouver. I order a pot of tea. Letting my tears flow freely, I pull out a pad of paper and begin to write.

My darling Jabir,

I've ordered a cup of Earl Grey tea in your honor (to rehydrate me after my tears) but I can't make tea the way you do. I don't know if I will ever send this letter, but it feels good to write, all the same. I don't want to make things any harder for you than they already are. This is painful for both of us, I know, and it is very sad and unsettling that things beyond our control are seeming to decide our fate in so personal and intimate a matter as our beautiful relationship. McGill has turned into an ugly place for me—the whole world, actually, looks a little darker today.

I care for you too deeply to hurt you, though—I don't ever want to be the cause of your pain or misfortune. It is this desire that allows me to let you go, as much as that hurts me. Both you and I are too precious to be exposed to such hatred—I can't let you go through life under the scrutiny and distrust of your friends and colleagues—you have a great future before you—you have been blessed with a brilliant mind coupled with important ideas to impart—that I could never stand in the way of.

What I'm trying to say is, I don't want to break up with you, Jabir, but I am forcing myself to. Because if I love you, which I may, then I must let you go.

This letter, I know deep down, is a way of saving face, a way of trying to sound selfless, like a hero. "Things beyond our control" isn't a lie, but neither is it totally true. If Jabir was truly dedicated to me, if his love and desire matched my own, he'd tell those students to fuck off. He'd realize they might even simply be envious of our connection. What I really feel like saying is, *I want you; I long for you; I need you. How can you leave me?*

CHAPTER 8

Orange Kinley

1983

"Ron, can you set the Betamax to tape *Fame* and *That's Incredible!?*" My dad had bought my mom and stepdad a VCR earlier this year as a gift, and I'm hoping to be able to catch up on my favorite shows when I get back from my trip to Israel. My baba is taking me there for three weeks.

The plan is that we will stay with my aunt and uncle on their kibbutz. I'm excited to finally see it for myself. In fourth grade, I had completed a school project on the topic of kibbutzim. In careful cursive on loose-leaf paper fastened together in an orange Duo-Tang, I wrote,

When Jewish immigrants moved to Israel, they had to buy desert land from the Arabs, had to work very hard, and on top of it all, they had to fight the Arabs. Therefore, they decided that it would be much easier if one person took care of the children, another person cooked, and a few others worked. Then, it would be much easier to survive.

I added little factoids to the top of each page, encircled in a cloud-like doodle:

Israel is about the same size as Lake Winnipeg.

and

Kibbutzim are put on the border to protect Israel.

© The Author(s) 2021
M. Sucharov, *Borders and Belonging: A Memoir*,
https://doi.org/10.1007/978-3-030-53732-6_8

91

and

Kibbutz children are taken on tours of the country, to help them learn to love Israel.

I've learned that every kibbutz has *agriculture* and an *industry*. My aunt and uncle's kibbutz has fish farms and a factory that produces pickles and olives. I like pickles—the salty dill kind and the little sweet gherkin kind that I eat on the side of deli sandwiches my dad makes me for lunch sometimes. But I don't really like olives, which I think of as more for adults. On the trip we will visit other extended family around the country and tour all the famous sites I've learned about in school. I can't wait.

Into my suitcase I fold my light-blue corduroy pants, my summer camp visor, my Jewish day school's 75th anniversary T-shirt, my white T-shirt with my face printed on it in tiny computer pixels, my red and orange flip-flops, my white Stan Smiths, my Judy Blume diary with two blue Bic pens, and my instamatic camera. Because we'll be there for Passover, attending the communal seder on the kibbutz, I make sure to add a fancy outfit: a red tartan matching skirt and blouse with lace edging.

My baba promises my mom that we will send telexes from the kibbutz office, to let her know how our trip is going. "Mirtz, make sure you take lots of pictures with you actually in them," my dad says. "I wanna see *you* in action." I nod and hug him goodbye.

This will be my first time in Israel, but my baba has been to Israel many times, even long before my aunt and uncle made aliya in 1973. She even went right before the 1956 War. For that, she made it into the newspaper.

The Vancouver Sun, November 8, 1956

City Mother Back from Middle East

Marian Margolis returned from the Middle East war theatre Wednesday. The attractive mother watched the Israeli parliament on the first day of the war and was huddled into an air-raid shelter at Lydda airport just before her evacuation from the Middle East.

She was greeted at the airport here by her husband...and three young daughters.

All had feared for her safety in Israel. When word she was safe arrived, Josephine, age four, asked:

"has she crossed the line? Is she bleeding?"

Mrs. Margolis entered Israel Oct. 11 for a seminar. The seminar was called off.

"The attitude of the people of Israel will assure its survival," said Mrs. Margolis. "They have indescribable courage and determination to save and build their state."

I've learned about all the Arab-Israeli wars for the JNF Israel contest we enter each year at school: 1948, 1956, 1967, 1973, 1982. There was also a War of Attrition somewhere in there, but I always forget when it was. The most recent war, between Israel and the PLO in Lebanon, was just last summer. As soon as I learn about it at school, I realize no one told us about it while we were at camp, and I'm a bit annoyed that we were kept out of the loop.

My baba tells me that my uncle was a reservist in the war in Lebanon. Since he's a dentist, I figure that he helped out at the clinic. Maybe it was even like *M*A*S*H*. I picture him going north from his kibbutz across the border to Lebanon, with the sound of helicopters overhead, while he helps the other soldiers with their teeth. Do soldiers need to see dentists? I'm not sure.

I'm not too scared about the possible wars. I'm more scared when I have to take the bus from my school every Thursday, down Main Street and through the rough part of the North End and then downtown to the YMHA for my Chai folk dance class. My cousin is the dance teacher, and she choreographs a dance for us to "Eye of the Tiger." Her parents and my parents are both divorced, and her dad is busy *getting his life back on track*. That's what my dad says when I ask him why we don't see them much, aside from dance class.

On the bus each week, drunk people sometimes get on and stumble toward me and I pray that they won't try to talk to me. I stare straight ahead while my insides go topsy-turvy and I count the stops until it's my turn to get off. Next to the YMHA, where I take my dance class, is my dad's old apartment with the melty painting.

Now, at the Winnipeg airport with my baba, all I can think of is that I can't wait to see Israel for real, to see Hebrew Coca-Cola labels close up and palm trees and the Mediterranean Sea and an actual desert. And I can't wait to speak Hebrew.

I turn to my baba, sitting next to me on the flight to Tel Aviv. "French is a much more beautiful language than Yiddish is."

While we were sitting in the Montreal airport lounge at Mirabel airport where we'd transferred from Winnipeg, a bat flew overhead in the airport lounge. I yelped and shielded my eyes. But now we're safe on the plane with many hours ahead of us, so I figure I might as well get a good debate going.

"How can you even compare the two languages?" my baba says. "Yiddish is the language of our people."

"But it has so many weird sounds. *A libe af dayn kop.*"

I exaggerate the Yiddish phrase I know best, the one I say to my great-grandmother to impress her when we visit her apartment, which is half independent and half assisted. Literally, it means *love on your head*, as in *bless your heart*.

"French, on the other hand, is *way* prettier. French is the language of love. *Bonjour mon ami.*" I try out my best faux-French accent and swirl my hands around my face.

I feel like a bit of an expert on the issue of languages because, at my school, we spend half a day in English and half a day in Hebrew, and a few hours every week learning French *and* Yiddish. Plus, I've been a contestant at the French poetry reciting contests around the city since grade one.

My baba scowls. I take a sip of my ginger ale.

"Anyway, if I had to choose a Jewish language, it would definitely be Hebrew," I say. "Yiddish is *so* old-fashioned."

She returns to her novel, something by Irwin Shaw, and I return to my Mad Libs, before falling asleep for the rest of the flight.

As we walk down the stairs of the plane at Ben Gurion airport, I bend down and touch the tarmac, like I've seen people do in movies. We are shepherded into the main terminal to retrieve our luggage. My eyes widen as I see vending machines with Hebrew letters. Orange Kinley soda. Coca-Cola. Hebrew pay phones where you put a little coin in called an *asimon*. I've seen some counselors at camp wearing them around their necks as a necklace charm and I immediately want one too.

When we arrive at my aunt and uncle's kibbutz, I examine the room I'll be sleeping in for the next three weeks. There's one bed for me and one for my baba. Last winter, I got to stay with my baba at her winter house in Palm Desert, which is near Palm Springs, but we always call it Palm Desert to be precise. There she took me to play tennis at her country club and I swam in her pool and sat in her jacuzzi and looked out over the concrete wall into the desert beyond and went for *cocktails* to her friends' houses and tried to teach myself how to play bridge so I could be a *fourth*.

At my baba's country club, I wanted to play in the youth tennis round-robin, but you had to know how to keep score and I didn't.

"Baba, can you teach me? Please? I've gotta learn right now. I promise to concentrate!"

"OK, sit down and get me a pen." She grabbed the napkin next to my iced tea, looked around, and found a golf pencil.

"Love is for zero. It comes from *l'oeuf*," she said. "An egg is shaped like a zero."

"You're right! That's cool." I knew the word *oeuf* from French class.

"And five is the nickname for fifteen. It's faster to say five-all than fifteen-all."

I nodded quickly, trying to take in all the information.

"After love and then fifteen, it goes straight to thirty and then to forty, and if it's a 40-40 tie, it's called deuce."

I'd heard the word deuce before, from the card game Acey-Deucey.

After deuce, you have to win by two points. So ad-in is when you, as the server, have won the point—advantage for you—and ad-out means an advantage for your opponent."

"Got it."

And "FBI means first ball in. It's a good way to warm up your serve. And don't forget tennis etiquette," she said. "Never cross behind someone else's court when a point is being played. Always have a second ball in your pocket when you're serving; no one wants to wait while you chase one down."

I took a final sip of my iced tea, straightened my Lacoste collar, adjusted my visor, and grabbed my racquet before running onto the court and into the waiting California sun.

At my baba's house in Palm Desert, I had my own room, where I filled in my Judy Blume diary before going to bed, recording the night we went out for dinner with her friends, and the day I cut my foot on a cactus.

This time, though, in Israel at my aunt and uncle's house, we will be roommates for three weeks. Just like at camp. I put my clothes away on the shelves my aunt has cleared for us in the built-in cupboards. I slip my pajamas under my pillow. I look over at my Baba and grin. "Are you hungry? Auntie made a delicious soup for us," my Baba says.

I'm not sure when my aunt and uncle are supposed to use their own kitchen and when they are supposed to eat in the dining hall. The dining hall reminds me of the *chadar ochel* at camp, except without the singing of cabin songs. I am intrigued by the unfamiliar soap scents in my aunt's bathroom, the toilets that flush strangely, and the pungent smell that wafts across the kibbutz from the cowshed.

At breakfast the next day, I fill my bowl with cream of wheat and top it with the hot milk that flows from a lever. For lunch, I eat chicken and rice and corn and pickles. We sit outside, at long tables set up on the balcony. We can see the grassy area where the kibbutzniks gather for concerts. As is often the case, my plate is too full, and I don't finish my food.

"Are you in the mood for a little adventure?" my aunt asks me. It's 8:30 p.m., already dark, and I am about to change into my pajamas for bed. "Let's take a stroll to the *chadar ochel*. We can get hot cocoa."

Except on Halloween, I rarely walk the streets of Winnipeg after dark, just for a stroll, even with my parents. But there are no robbers or muggers here on the kibbutz. A wave of warmth washes over me. The next day is Friday, and that evening, I help my aunt push the dinner cart around the dining hall. On Friday nights, for Shabbat, the kibbutzniks get table service rather than having to stand in line with their trays.

"It's called *toranut*, work rotation," my aunt explains.

"Oh, I know all about *toranut*. We have it at camp. Except at camp the *toranim* don't use carts. We stand in pairs in a long row, waiting to sing *hamotzi*, and then we go to the kitchen and carry trays of food to our cabin's table and then clear the dishes afterwards."

My aunt nods with interest. Her eyes sparkle back with excitement at my own chatty description of camp.

As I walk around with my aunt and the cart, I stand up straight and look each person in the eye. "*Atem rotzim marak?*" I ask. Do you want soup? My aunt talks fancy Hebrew: *Hayitem rotzim marak?* Would you like soup? Mostly I speak Hebrew the way I've learned it at Jewish school and at camp, but I still try to make it sound as fancy as I can.

The next night, my uncle invites me to accompany him on guard duty, *shmira*. I know that word too, from camp, where counselors guard the girls side from the boys side and vice versa, though the boys still manage to visit our cabin sometimes.

I'm not sure who we are guarding against on the kibbutz, but I figure it might have something to do with the Arabs who live in the nearby villages, like I wrote about in my fourth-grade kibbutz project. The counselors at camp had no weapons. Only flashlights. I figure my uncle probably has a gun in that booth but I don't really want to know either way.

In the afternoons, I play cards and backgammon with my teenage cousins. We visit my aunt's friends on the neighboring kibbutz and attend a symphony concert on the lawn of our own. I visit the English library so I can pick out a book. There, I spot Chaim Potok's *The Chosen*. My aunt signs it out for me and I clutch it to my chest. I saw the movie five times in the downtown Winnipeg cineplex just last month. I love the parts where Danny is studying Talmud and twirling his *payos*, his sidelocks. I love the relationship between Reuven and his Dad, who reminds me a bit of my dad.

"There are two famous actors in the movie, Mira," my dad had said.

"Yeah, Danny was in *Ice Castles*. And Reuven was in *Fame!*"

"Oh, that's right! But those aren't the ones I mean. The two fathers are very famous. One is named Rod Steiger and the other is Maximillian Schell. Actually, you already know Maximillian Schell from *The Black Hole*." I loved *The Black Hole*. He was so different in that, I hardly recognize him.

My uncle takes us to visit a Jaffa grapefruit factory, and on the way I snap a photo of a Hebrew Coca-Cola truck out of our car window. On our way to Masada, we stop by the side of the highway to take a picture with a boy, who my aunt explains is an Arab, along with his mother and their donkey. So that's what Arabs look like, I think.

As April 1 rolls around, there is no one in Israel to mark April Fool's with. My aunt explains that Purim, rather than April Fool's, is when Israelis get silly and do jokes and spoofs. I know about costumes on Purim—this year I went as a greaser and wore a leather vest over a white T-shirt and rolled a box of Popeye cigarettes under my sleeve like Schneider on *One Day at a Time*. I wanted to slick back my hair but I didn't know about hair gel yet, so I used Vaseline. It took a long time to get it out. It looked super cool, though. Since there's no one to play April Fool's jokes on, I tell my diary about the special day instead.

On quiet afternoons, we play rounds of the first grown-up board game I've seen. It's called Trivial Pursuit and it has little plastic pies with colorful wedges you get when you answer a question right. Even though I don't know many of the answers, I love taking educated guesses. I've learned about educated guesses in school. My favorite category is pink: entertainment. My best category is green: science and nature. And then, when I am getting bored of being the only kid around, and no one feels like playing Trivial Pursuit with me anymore, they send me to join the kibbutz kids at their school for a week.

"Watch out, she knows Hebrew," one tall girl with a broad build says to no one in particular, as she smooths the hair off her face. I love listening to these Israeli kids speak the language I know only from school and camp. I love how they start their day eating breakfast together, after they've woken up together in the children's house where they sleep, four to a room. They show me their small metal beds. The beds remind me of ours at camp, except that these ones are topped with real blankets rather than sleeping bags.

I love accompanying their class on hikes during the school subject they call *teva*, nature. I love playing pickup basketball with them in the afternoons and accompanying their team to an inter-kibbutz basketball championship to cheer them on, and eating rectangles of ice cream sliced from a box when my aunt and grandmother come to host a goodbye party for me. The teacher presents me with a small hardcover Hebrew book that she has inscribed with a message from the class.

One afternoon during that trip to Israel, my aunt and uncle drop my teenage cousin, her friend, and me off in Afula, a town twenty kilometers away. In the spring heat, we walk the narrow streets to a little salon so my cousin's friend can get her ears pierced. I'm too scared to think about getting my own ears pierced. Then they buy me ice cream. When it's time to return to the kibbutz, my cousin leads us away from the town center to the edge of the main road.

"Stick out your arm," she says. "Someone will stop and give us a ride."

My stomach begins twisting in knots and I feel a hot flash wash over me.

"I really don't think that's a good idea," I say. "I'm not supposed to hitchhike." I kick at the gravel with my toe.

"This is Israel, not Canada. This is what we do here. Everything will be fine." My cousin looks away, toward the approaching cars.

My eyes dart from her to the road and back again.

A couple of minutes later, a car pulls up. It's someone my cousin knows from the kibbutz. He loads us into his car and drives us back to safety.

"See Mira? I told you everything would be fine." She's rolling her eyes.

"I'm not supposed to hitchhike," I say again quietly.

The next day, my grandmother takes my other cousin and me to Tel Aviv. I notice from billboards around town that Kids from Fame is performing live that night in the local stadium. I love Kids from Fame more than anything. I have their album and I listen to it all the time. I love the song "Friday Night's Gonna Be Alright" and the fast-moving "High Fidelity." I love singing and dancing along in my room.

"Please Baba, can we go to the concert? You'll love it! They are so awesome."

"Not this time," she says. I know there won't be a next time. In Winnipeg, we don't get big concerts like Kids from Fame.

"Why don't you walk over to the main hotels on the beach?" my baba suggests. "Maybe you'll see them and at least you can get an autograph."

My cousin leads me down the promenade to see if we can find the Kids from Fame. But we only see Israelis and tourists. The day after the concert, my grandmother takes me to a Tel Aviv record store to buy a copy of the *Fame* album for my cousins. I'm not quite sure how this is consolation.

That night, as we are walking along the beach, the memorial day siren sounds. We stand at attention. I'm looking at the ground, trying to appear solemn. I try hard to think about what it means to be a soldier or what it means to lose a loved one in a war. The Jewish high schoolers in Winnipeg sing about Israeli soldiers going off to war at the annual Song Festival. Next year, I hope to enter the same song festival, since I'll be in sixth grade, the first year we're eligible. Maybe I'll write a song about war too, now that I've been to Israel.

The only war veterans I ever saw in Canada were the old men in the shopping malls with missing limbs, the ones who made my guts swirl when I was younger. Here, everyone is a soldier. Even my uncle and cousin.

I guess the Arabs who my uncle is guarding the kibbutz against aren't soldiers. But if they are trying to attack the kibbutz, maybe they are soldiers for *their side*? I'm not really sure whose side is whose, since we saw an Arab boy and his mom and donkey walking along the side of the road in Israel when we stopped for a photo last week. But there aren't any Arabs on the kibbutz. So maybe they *are* the other side.

The next morning we meet an older, distant relative named Henya for breakfast. I pose with her for a picture on the beachfront boardwalk. With her short stature, tweed suit, and Eastern European name, I conjure a fantasy of her having made it to Israel by escaping Europe by boat. She doesn't speak much English, and I try to talk to her in my best Hebrew.

At the Tel Aviv cafe, they don't have breakfast items on the menu, so my baba lets me order a cup of tea and a bowl of ice cream. I stick my spoon into the ice cream and sip my tea, letting the hot and cold mix and melt in my mouth and tickle my teeth. Hot, Cold. Hot. Cold. *cham. kar.* I promise myself I'll write about my special breakfast later that night in my diary. My friends back home won't believe it when I tell them.

A few days after our stay in Tel Aviv, we reach Jerusalem. "We were led to the bus depot by a handsome Israeli soldier," I write in my diary the next night. When I read it back a few months later, I realize that someone—my grandmother or my aunt—must have told me to write about the *handsome soldier*. Normally, I use the word cute, never handsome. Cute is what we call the actors—like Ricky Schroder and Ralph Macchio—whose photos we clip from *Tiger Beat* and pin up in our rooms, like at my dad's cottage near camp where I go to the drugstore on the main strip of town and stock up on candy and teen magazines. I wonder if Israeli fifth-graders have pictures of soldiers in *their* teen magazines.

At the Kotel, my baba drapes my head in a blue cotton shawl, and I grasp at an urgent sense of piousness as I recite the Shema before placing a note between the cracks. I hate being forced to pray every morning in my Jewish day school, where the teachers walk up and down the aisles to make sure our mouths are moving. But I like tefillah at camp, where we get to choose the tunes to "Adon Olam." Tunes like "Jimmy Crack Corn" and the slow, emotional tune that Chai, the local folk troupe, sings on their album, and that I like to sing in my best singing voice when I am in the bath. Here in Israel, at the Kotel, tefillah feels good too. Maybe this is even what holy feels like, I think. I stroke the stones, feeling their smooth edges and then their pointy parts, and squint against the strong sun reflected off the plaza as I follow my baba out toward the rest of the Old City.

At Yad Vashem, I snap pictures of the black iron sculptures that adorn the grounds, trying to take in the enormity of the Holocaust. I've learned about the concentration camps in school. I saw footage of naked concentration camp victims in the part of *The Chosen* where Reuven is sitting in a theater watching a movie and the newsreel part comes on. No one in my family that I know of died in the Holocaust. But I've read *Chernowitz* by Fran Arrick, one of my favorite books, and I know antisemitism can strike anywhere. Even now.

At Caesaria, I strike a pose for the camera in the Roman amphitheater. It's like the *bamu* at camp, the outdoor stage where we sometimes do little shows and to which we've given a funny nickname to distinguish it from the indoor *bama*. At the tip of the Kinneret, wearing the shorts, T-shirt, and flip-flops that will accompany me back to summer camp three months later, I pose serenely so my parents can see where I've been.

On April 18 this year, it's Israeli independence day: Yom Ha'atzma'ut. There's a huge carnival on the kibbutz. My uncle guides me toward the rides that have been set up for the evening. "Try the zip line," he says.

"I don't usually like rides," I say.

"Try it. You just might like it. It's not scary."

I climb onto the scaffolding that has been set atop the expansive lawn, grab the metal handles as instructed, and let my feet propel me off the platform. My insides swoosh just the right amount as I slide along the cable and reach the other side, where I land squarely on the platform. I climb down and immediately line up for another turn. This ride is perfect. It must have been made just for me.

"That was the best Yom Ha'atzma'ut I have ever experienced," I tell my Judy Blume diary, carefully rendering the Hebrew letters with my ballpoint pen and almost getting the spelling right.

During this time, peace between Israel and Egypt is still fresh and Israelis are beginning to display some curiosity toward their former enemy. Riding this wave of possibility, my grandmother and I plan to fly to Cairo for a few days. I am excited by the prospect. Our relatives pack our suitcases with boxes of crackers, bottles of water, and cans of tuna. But at the last minute my grandmother sighs, "I don't think we should go," she says. "It's too far, and it's dangerous. I don't want to get sick. And I don't want you to get sick." She tousles my hair.

The idea of Egypt felt both exotic and scary, and I can't decide which feeling is stronger: relief or disappointment. My grandmother and I stay in Israel and have dinner with our other relatives in Ramat Gan. "Steak with tehina? Or falafel?" my cousin asks. I look to my baba for answers; I'm not sure if I like either of those things.

"Try the steak," my cousin says to me. "It's delicious."

So my cousin goes to pick up steaks in pita slathered with tehina from a local restaurant and brings them back for us wrapped in paper and tin foil. I stare at the sandwiches. I don't usually like creamy sauces, but I want to like this meal that my cousin has brought back. I try to chat affably with my relatives while I pick at the edges of my pita and sip from a bottle of lemon Kinley and pose for photographs with these cousins, using my best smile.

Instead of taking an El Al flight to Cairo, we take an Egged bus back to the kibbutz. About half an hour into the ride, we look down and see a thin puddle of orange liquid flowing toward our bags.

"Pick up your bags, Mira!" My baba is grabbing my arm.

We soon realize what has happened. The teenage boy sitting four rows behind us—he looks like an Israeli, not a tourist—has thrown up. My baba and I look at each other, our eyes wide, and squeal with laughter.

A year later almost to the day, Israel will be reeling from the Bus 300 affair, where members of the Shin Bet execute two Palestinians who have hijacked an Egged bus. It will be the same kind of Egged bus I rode with my grandmother when that teenager threw up. That bus was headed from Tel Aviv to Ashkelon, ours from Tel Aviv to Afula. And six years later, another tragedy—one that touches the Winnipeg Jewish community directly—will happen on an Israeli bus, a tragedy I'll learn of that summer at camp.

And thirty-three years after that, the last lucid conversation my baba and I will have—right before her mind dissolves in her mid-nineties, and her body a few months later, will be about that episode on the bus with the boy and our suitcases and the contents of his stomach. We will share a laugh and my heart will swell with love. A few months later, when I am visiting her in her apartment, lying on her bed while she lies on the rented hospital bed we have moved into her bedroom for her final weeks, and before I take her hand and sing Hebrew songs to soothe her, she will call urgently to her caregiver, point to me, and say, "Who is that and why is she still among us?"

When I return to my fifth-grade classroom at Jewish day school that spring, the principal calls me aside. "We would love for you to give a presentation about your wonderful trip to Israel," she says, emphasizing *wonderful*.

"Sure, I would love to."

I stand up straighter and smile. My mind flickers back over all my adventures, trying to decide which places and stories I will highlight.

My friends will probably like hearing about the kids on the kibbutz and their basketball tournament. And the vomit on the bus of course. And my almost-trip to Egypt that didn't actually happen. And how I almost met the Kids from *Fame*. And maybe even the new board game called Trivial Pursuit. And the orange Kinley and the *asimons* and the Hebrew Coca-Cola signs that are all over the place. And how Israelis actually celebrate Yom Ha'atzma'ut with outdoor carnivals and zip lines. And the weird steak with creamy sauce. And my breakfast of tea and ice cream. And how there were no wars while we were there but I did almost have to hitchhike from Afula to the kibbutz, though thankfully a man from the kibbutz saved us from getting kidnapped and murdered.

As I construct the talk in my head, I revel in the knowledge that my classmates who have missed school for a spring trip to Hawaii or Florida or Disneyland or Palm Springs have not been invited to do the same.

In sixth grade, I sit with Gil, a boy from school, in his bedroom. A few months earlier, Gil and I had decided to "go around." Gil has a leather-upholstered waterbed and his bedroom walls are plastered with movie posters. We are there to work on an end-of-year project on the Knesset for Hebrew class. Gil is Israeli. Well, he was born in Israel. His parents brought him to Canada when he was a year old, around the Yom Kippur War, in 1973. I recall the month and year of all the wars from the Jewish National Fund Israel contest last year.

We've learned a little about the Knesset in school, but we want to do well on the project and so we gather as much new information as we can get. We phone Gil's grandparents, who still live in Israel. It's eight hours later there, in Ramat Gan, and they've just finished dinner. Holding the phone to his ear, Gil passes along the information to me and I take notes. Yitzhak Shamir is prime minister. They explain that he took over the year before from Menachem Begin, who got sick. The Likud holds 48 seats in the 120-seat Knesset; the Alignment, also known as Labor, has 47. The rest of the seats are divided among the smaller parties. They tell us more about the history of some of the parties and I write furiously.

We write up our findings in Hebrew, in a blue Duo-Tang, and hand it proudly to our teacher the next day. At our elementary school graduation a week later, Gil and I share the award for top student in General Studies and Judaic Studies. Our prize is Chaim Potok's book *Wanderings*, with our name calligraphied inside the front cover. As I approach the podium to accept my award, my English teacher leans in to kiss my cheek and I scan the room for my parents' camera. The result is a photo where my eyes are reaching as far to the side as they can go.

Soon after graduation, in the week between school and camp, Gil and I walk to the corner store near our school and buy two bottles of Grape Crush. The storekeeper removes the caps for us. We usually drink from cans. But today we're drawn to these old-fashioned bottles. We sip our crush and head back to the school, walking side by side. The streets are quiet save for an occasional passing car. Sunlight is enveloping us and the early summer Manitoba caterpillars are out. We are quiet, until Gil turns to me. "Do you wanna hold hands?" he asks.

A few weeks earlier, my parents had dropped us off at the movie theater downtown to see *Indiana Jones and the Temple of Doom*. Half an hour into the movie, Gil leaned toward me. "Can I hold your hand?" he whispered.

I really wanted him to hold my hand. But instead of saying yes, I said, "Are you crazy?" I immediately regretted it and my heart beat wildly. But since I'd said no, all that was left for me to do was eat my popcorn and Junior Mints and struggle to concentrate on Harrison Ford until the theater lights went on again.

"Sure," I say now, as we continue walking back to school. Gil takes my left hand in his. His grasp is soft and strong. His hands aren't sweaty like I've read about in *Then Again, Maybe I Won't*. They are pleasantly smooth. I interlace my fingers in his.

At the end of the year, after I've told all my friends that I'm moving to Vancouver at the end of the summer, Gil hands me a wallet-size school photo. On the back, in delicate script, he has written, "I will always remember you."

Nine years later, I will be at Hebrew University, finishing off a study-abroad year program. Gil, who is passing through Jerusalem on a summer visit to his grandparents and cousins, will contact me, and I'll invite him to join me and my university friends at a restaurant where I'm presented with a slice of cake topped with a sparkler. After we toast with Israeli wine and eat the cake, Gil will hand me a paperback copy of Edward Said's *Orientalism*. He'd seen me admire it while we were browsing in the English-language bookstore that afternoon. Opening the front cover, I'll recognize his handwriting from the letters we exchanged when we were kids, and, later, teens.

Dear Mira,

On the unexpected surprise to celebrate your 21st birthday with you, here's to your continuing academic success,

With love,

Gil

CHAPTER 9

Buses and Cars

1994

My head jerks forward, jolting me awake. I glance at the soldier sitting next to me; he's around my age, maybe a little younger. Dark hair, crew cut. The long nose of his rifle—with such a long gun, he must still be junior in the ranks—is pointed toward the floor. I hope I haven't accidentally let my head rest on his shoulder. It's nearing 8:30 a.m., and I am still sleepy from catching the Egged bus an hour earlier in Tel Aviv after a late night out with my roommates.

I look out the window as the Jerusalem buildings come into view. Soon, the bus stops and I get off at the central bus station and approach a snack kiosk. "*Boker tov. Shtei Mento, bevakasha.*" Good morning, two packs of Mentos, please.

I've learned to keep English nouns singular when speaking Hebrew, even if I'm ordering two packs of Mentos, as I am this morning. Nor do you really have to say "packs of" in Hebrew. I'm trying to speak in a lower register and adopt the particular vocal swagger that I hear Israelis use. I clutch the rolls of candy in my palm: one mint and one mixed fruit. I pop the candies into my mouth, one by one, and chew them quickly, willing myself to wake up. I have a long day at the Knesset ahead of me, plus the commute back to Tel Aviv.

I had secured the barely paid Knesset internship—entailing commuting from Tel Aviv three days a week, with bus fare eating up most of

© The Author(s) 2021

M. Sucharov, *Borders and Belonging: A Memoir*,
https://doi.org/10.1007/978-3-030-53732-6_9

my modest paycheck—with a smile and a handshake in my grandmother's living room a couple of months earlier. She was hosting a Jewish Federation event in Vancouver with a visiting dignitary, a Knesset member.

"*Na'im me'od*," I said to the MK. Nice to meet you.

"I've just finished my degree in Middle East Studies. I'm heading to Israel next month, actually, for the year."

"Oh, wonderful," he said.

"Might you have any openings in your office? I would be honored to intern for you."

A month later, everything was in place.

But first I had to get my Knesset security pass. In a small trailer adjacent to the main building, I sat across from a middle-aged security officer with a tanned, lined face and close-cropped salt and pepper hair.

"Are you on any medications?" he asked.

"Um, no. Well, I *have* been on the birth control pill before. And sometimes I need prescription skin cream."

"Have you ever seen a psychologist?"

"When I was younger. After my parents' divorce."

"How old were you when your parents separated?"

"Three and a half."

"*Mizkena*," he said, poor kid. He smiled sympathetically. His eyes said, we're all family here. If your grandparents had come to Palestine instead of to Canada, you could have been my daughter.

"Come to think of it, I also saw a therapist for some anxiety when I was in eighth grade. It's not a big deal. My dad is a psychiatrist. It's something we do in my family. I understand that Israelis are also very open to psychotherapy. You know, Jews and psychoanalysis, and all that. Sigmund Freud!" Now I was rambling.

He scribbled some notes on a clipboard. I shifted in my seat.

A few days later, my security clearance arrived.

Still chewing on my Mentos, I catch a city bus near the central terminal, and ten minutes later I'm flashing my security pass and walking through the turnstile up the grand plaza toward the Knesset building. On the way to the new wing, where my MK's office is housed, I pass a series of framed portraits of Israel's founding leaders. A thrill passes through me, as it does every time I'm here.

I pass the marble plaza with the small café; I'm already picturing my mid-morning snack of grilled cheese on pita. I glance toward

Bibi Netanyahu's door as I walk by. A couple of weeks earlier, I'd received a letter from my grandmother, who knew I was interning in the Knesset. Would I please get an autographed photo of Bibi for her husband, Joe, who was a big fan? So the next day, I'd knocked on the door. "Just so you know," I told Bibi's assistant, as I accepted the photo from her, "I don't share your boss's politics." She shot me a bored look. I had first heard of Bibi in 1988 as I was sitting with my boyfriend Gil on his waterbed. "My grandparents love this new Israeli political up-and-comer," he had said. "Binyamin Netanyahu is his name. He's really going to shake things up over there."

Occasionally, I get to work on something substantial—researching comparative law around minimum mandatory sentencing, say, but as an intern, I mostly send faxes, distribute press releases in the journalists' cubbies, and gossip with the main parliamentary assistant. When she told me her parents were from Tunisia, I stopped short. "Really?" I said. "I didn't realize you were Mizrahi!"

"Why are you so surprised?" she bristled.

I turned red, realizing my misstep. She had caught me in a tacit assumption that to be Ashkenazi is normal, and to be Mizrahi is to be Other. Her hair was dyed bright red, obscuring her natural, presumably darker color; she didn't use the Mizrahi pronunciation of the letters "het" and "ayin"; and she seemed like many of the Ashkenazi relatives I had in Israel. I prayed that she wouldn't think me a racist.

"Oh, no reason ... I just assumed." I trailed off awkwardly, and we settled into our cafeteria meal of couscous with mixed vegetables, mumbling pleasantries to a mayor's driver sitting nearby.

Today, As I enter my MK's office, I spot this assistant, sporting a wrist full of gold bangles, looking tense. Her ashtray already contains the remnants of two cigarettes, and she's holding a third between her long red nails as she looks anxiously at the TV news. On the screen, I see images of a charred Egged bus. Underneath the footage, the words flash: "Attack in Tel Aviv. Bus number 5." I know the buses well enough by now to know that the number 5 runs along Dizengoff Street, downtown.

The dead and wounded are being carried away on stretchers atop the ticker-tape announcements running for viewers who've just tuned in. Police officers have surrounded the scene. Magen David Adom ambulances line the perimeter. White plastic chairs sit overturned near the burnt bus, carried there from their perch in front of sidewalk cafés through the force of the blast. Sappers with vests and helmets scour the wreckage for undetonated bombs. And soon, in accordance with Jewish law, volunteers from ZAKA will be on the scene to collect bits of flesh so that no bodily parts are left behind.

I swallow hard. It could have been me being carried off on a stretcher. It might still be me, on another bus on another day with another terrorist carrying explosives strapped to his body. I mentally calculate the distance between the spot of the bombing—Dizengoff Square, near the colorful Agam fountain I love—and my own apartment on Mazeh Street. Less than three kilometers.

We learn that twenty-two people have been killed and another fifty have been injured. One of the dead is from the Netherlands. Another is only twenty years old, nearly exactly my age, and is from my aunt and uncle's kibbutz in the north. I know my parents will see the news on CNN and will worry. So I phone my mom to let her know I'm fine.

"Do you think I should come home?" I ask, trying to mask the fear in my voice.

"Stay," she says. "You've got to live your life."

I'm partly relieved. I want to be in Israel so badly this year. After spending the year at Hebrew University two years ago, when I went back to McGill for my final year of undergrad, all I wanted to do was figure out how to return to Israel. I wanted to come back here—despite how my second-to-last full day in Israel had turned out.

Two days before I was scheduled to return to Canada, with final exams at Hebrew University nearly over, the professor at the research institute where I'd been interning invited me to lunch. To thank me for my work, he said. The plan was that he would pick me up on the Mount Scopus campus and we'd drive to a restaurant in the city center. But at the last minute, he phoned me.

"I'd rather not be stuck in traffic and then have to sit in a hot restaurant downtown. Let's drive to Abu Ghosh instead." Abu Ghosh was a neighborhood on the outskirts of the city. It was breezier there, but also more isolated. I preferred the first plan. Downtown was my comfort zone. I knew the shops and restaurants. The streets were busy and well populated. But I said, "Sure, that sounds fine."

On the ride there, the silences were becoming awkward. I was used to sitting and talking with him, in his office, about the research project. But those conversations were always pretty formal. He was quiet and reserved, and I didn't especially connect with him. I valued the internship experience, and I respected him as a supervisor, but I didn't find his research topic particularly fascinating. Nor did I find him particularly interesting. "How is the book coming?" I asked.

"It's coming along well," he said. "Thank you for your wonderful research on it."

I asked him about his next project, about how he decided to get into academia, about the institute. At lunch, I inquired after his wife and kids. But he didn't seem to want to talk much about them.

He eyed me curiously. "Were you a happy child?"

I was used to being as pleasant, polite, and articulate as I could be. I was used to answering questions forthrightly. Even personal ones.

So, between bites of eggplant and falafel and humous, I told him about my parents' divorce, how I'd coped by adopting an optimistic exterior and burying myself in my schoolwork and extracurricular activities. How I was outgoing and social. How I always loved to keep busy. It was probably a coping mechanism, I explained. He kept his eyes locked on my face. And then I told him about my impressions of the year in Israel, how I hoped to return, maybe intern in the Knesset, and then do graduate work in political science and maybe even pursue international law. "I'd love to work on Israeli-Palestinian negotiations," I said.

"Has Israel changed you?" he asked.

I considered the question. I wasn't altogether in the mood to continue down this more personal path, but I liked thinking about these things.

"It must have, but I don't know exactly how," I said. "I've probably become more relaxed, through meeting new people and having so many new experiences. It makes a person more flexible, you know?"

He nodded as a beat passed. "Are you a relaxed-type person?" he asked. And then he looked down. "Sorry for asking so many personal questions. It's just that I feel like I can."

"No, it's fine," I said. "Yeah, I guess I am a relaxed-type person."

I should have suggested we go—I still had lots to do back in my dorm, between the last of my exams and errands and packing—but I decided to introduce another topic.

"I'm pretty steadfast in my morals and views. That's one thing I've come across in Israeli society that has troubled me: the lack of progressivism, the sexism and the racism. But maybe that's just kibbutzniks. Maybe city life is different. More sophisticated. More cosmpolitan."

Not long before, some American friends and I had gone to see the Elton John concert in Tel Aviv's Yarkon Park, along with some friends from the kibbutz. I'd been so looking forward to it, especially being with real-life Israelis, real-life kibbutzniks, doing something that we all enjoyed. I'd been hoping that Gitai would be there, and that I'd get a sense of closure. I wanted to attend this gathering so much that I declined an invitation to the wedding of a family friend from Canada. I'd later learn that another Canadian—a guy named Steve, visiting Israel from Vancouver for his friend's wedding—would be there. Steve would later become my husband. And while I did happen to bump into him and another friend, who I did know, on Ben Yehuda in Jerusalem that week and was quickly introduced, it would take me another year to meet him properly, since what I most wanted that night was to hang out with Israelis.

The Elton John concert was exciting and fun, until the kibbutzniks we were with got drunk and began yelling homophobic slurs.

A few weeks before that, at the kibbutz disco, I was talking with another soldier friend from the kibbutz. Suddenly he pointed to a woman across the room. "Shit! She's so big," he said.

"Hey! Where do you think women get their fucked-up body image problems from?" I said in English. Then I switched to Hebrew. "It's from people with stupid ideas like these! What do you care if she's big or not? You don't even know her!"

"I'm not saying she's not nice," he said. "She might be really nice. I'm just saying that because of her appearance, I wouldn't bother to get to know her."

The conversation petered out fast.

A week later, another soldier friend and I were hanging out at the kibbutz disco. I brought up the conversation I'd had with his friend about the woman.

"Yeah, I heard," he said. And then he launched into a defense of his friend. "Don't you sometimes think impolite things? Like if you see a black person, don't you have to hold yourself back from saying 'fuckin' n—-?"

I was stunned into silence. I knew about Israelis' brusque style. Dugri, they call it. Arabic slang for straight talk. I often found it refreshing. Charming, even. But now the cultural gaps were turning into yawning chasms.

Still, I wanted the closeness I sometimes found with Israelis. A month earlier, these two friends had taken me on a short hike in the Wadi near the kibbutz. They made Turkish coffee in a small finjan and we snacked on Elite chocolate and sunflower seeds. Sprawled on the sand in our makeshift picnic spot, I realized there was no place I'd rather be. It wasn't so much the content of our conversation that afternoon as the fact that it was me they'd chosen to spend the afternoon with, and the fact that, after a year of awkward crushes and wrestling with Labor Zionist principles, I had made what felt like some truly good friends.

A few days after the awkward conversation about body shaming and racism, I was riding on the back of that friend's dirt bike, hearing the roar of the motor dulled by the helmet covering my ears, and feeling the wind on my face, breathing in the desert dustiness, passing Bedouin tents and herds of sheep along the way, our speed contrasting with the animals' languidness. I hadn't felt this free since riding the zip line on my aunt and uncle's kibbutz on Yom Ha'atzma'ut in 1983. And before that, at my dad's cottage in Sandy Hook, where I'd stand on top of an overturned purple inflatable dingy, waiting for the soft waves of Lake Winnipeg at dusk to overturn me, half-hoping to stay up forever, and half wanting to be dumped into the waiting waters. And before that, when I was five, and my dad let go of the seat of my bike and I pedaled furiously across the empty schoolyard of Gladstone school, powering my yellow bike with my own steam for the very first time. And later, when I was eight, and I'd spend late summer evenings riding my blue Sekine ten-speed around the flat prairie streets of my South Winnipeg neighborhood—after Dimitri had left our lives and Ron had entered. Niagara. Mathers Bay. Ash. Oak. Elm. Parallel roads with perfect back lanes ensured that there were no cars backing out of driveways to interrupt my flow. And the simple grid pattern meant I couldn't get lost.

Hanging out with my Israeli friend and a few others, I tried to cut through the tension. "You must hate us," I said. "First we come to your kibbutz when we're eighteen and fuck your brains out." I was referring to the gap year program my friends had gone on. "And then we return a couple of years later and tell you how to talk and how to think."

He mustered a laugh. So did I. And we went back to listening to Seal and chewing on sunflower seeds.

The internship advisor paid the bill at the restaurant and we headed back to his car. He turned to me. "Do you want to take a little drive through the mountains?"

I didn't want to. "I don't think I can," I said. "I have to get to the travel agent before they close."

But he persisted. "A short ride."

I looked at the ground, uneasy, and nodded halfheartedly. We drove a few miles along a deserted road in the hills. Suddenly, he pulled the car onto the shoulder, and we headed toward a small spring lined with stones.

My heart was beating quickly. I wanted to leave. I wanted to be safe in my dorm room. Packing. Preparing to fly back to Canada. Saying goodbye to my friends. But I followed him out of the car, toward the spring. Fortunately, there were several others at the site, enjoying the cool water. But as soon as he saw them, he turned abruptly back toward the car. I followed, my eyes downcast.

"Let's go to one more," he said.

I said nothing.

He drove along an even more deserted mountain road. I was gripping my armrest and staring straight ahead while I tried to keep him in my peripheral vision. He stopped the car, peered down into the valley, and said, "We don't have time to go down there."

Then he maneuvered the car dangerously along the cliff's edge. Now I was doubly frightened.

After a few more minutes of driving in silence, he stopped the car again, in the middle of the road. He pulled up the emergency brake and turned to me. "Can I kiss you goodbye?" he asked.

My heart raced. I sat there, frozen. The strange vibes I'd been getting from him had materialized into what I'd most dreaded.

"No," I sputtered. I reached for the door handle, knowing I had nowhere to go.

"Sorry," he said. "Just a friendly kiss."

I did not want to antagonize him, so I did what I do best: I talked. "I guess I misinterpreted," I began. "Maybe it's cultural differences." I was stalling for time, trying to bring the exchange back to the academic register in which I was most comfortable.

"Did I frighten you when I took you driving on this mountain road?" he asked.

I said nothing.

We drove on. After a few minutes, I said, "Let me off." We'd reached an empty bus stop along the edge of the highway. While I didn't know how I would get home if he did let me out, I wanted nothing more than to get out of this car.

"I'm not going to hurt you," he said. "Just stay in the car. I promise I'll take you right back to the campus. What time does the travel agency close?"

A few minutes later, we were passing through Castel National Park and I spotted a rest stop and a restaurant. "Stop the car," I said. This time, I was firm. "I'm getting out."

"No one wants to hurt you," he said. "In two minutes we'll be on the highway and I'll take you right home. Here you'll never get home!"

But I opened the door, climbed out, and exhaled. For the first time since the episode had begun to unfold, I felt safe.

"May I say something?" he asked, and I nodded. "I apologized already. It must be cultural differences."

Annoyed with myself for having fed him that cultural-differences fodder for an excuse, I shrugged. "Now is the time for me to change the course of the situation." I shut the car door and made my way to the restaurant ahead.

"Excuse me," I said to a waiter, my voice shaking. "Can you please call me a taxi?" The taxi driver brought me the thirteen kilometers back to my dorm room at Mount Scopus, where I handed him thirty shekels.

For years this episode sat with me like a lead ball wedged in my back pocket, dragging me down and drenching me in shame. It was the first intimate story I felt compelled to tell Steve, unburdening myself on one of our early dates. tossing the lead ball to someone else to hold, examine, and carry around so I no longer had to.

Now, talking to my mom on the day of the bus attack, I'm a tiny bit disappointed not to have the decision made for me to come home and am mostly glad she has encouraged me to stay. While I'm scared, I also long to be part of Israel. And that means staying. Even if there are terror attacks in the city in which I live.

A week later, the national mood lifts a little as Israel signs a peace treaty with Jordan.

This time, rather than watching the Washington, DC signing ceremony from a friend's apartment in Montreal, I tune into the Rabin-Hussein ceremony, taking place in the Arava, from a cafe in Tel Aviv. It feels like a new era, with the hope for peace and the threat of death—for me, first from the sun, with my melanoma scare a permanent part of my life now, and for all of us living here, with the threat of suicide bombs ever present.

A few years after the fax incident—when my aunt wondered why I was having the Palestinian National Authority send her missives—my aunt and uncle decide to leave the kibbutz for another gated community nearby.

Those communities have made headlines in Israel for their admissions committees, which tend to bar Arab citizens from moving in, using the morally dubious criteria of "social suitability" to assess applicants. I am careful not to use the term gated community when I talk to them in English. In Hebrew, it's called *Moshav shitufi*, a communal settlement, the term scrubbed of its suburban, racially segregated American connotations.

My aunt and uncle don't want to discuss any of this with me anyway. I'd probably get self-righteous and they'd probably become defensive. I struggle to keep my own hypocrisy in check anyway, and to make sure I'm aware of my own blinders. The all-Jewish kibbutzim that I loved when I was in my twenties—and which I helped my uncle guard from intruders when I was ten, and still visit now when I see my old "kibbutz family" who have since moved to a different kibbutz in the Negev—are just as gated.

Several months after the fax incident, I am returning on the evening bus from my aunt and uncle's kibbutz to Tel Aviv. I've enjoyed a relaxing weekend with them, enjoying the break from my weekday research duties at the Tel Aviv university library. As I settle into a book for the long ride back, the familiar beeping announcing the hourly news comes over the radio, and the driver raises the volume so the passengers can hear the newscast. The broadcaster is talking about an attack in Oklahoma. Many casualties. Terrorism.

I look down at the book I'm reading: *The Islamic Threat: Myth or Reality?* by John Esposito. This year, I've been devouring as many Middle East politics books as I can, trying to prepare for graduate school. Suddenly, my cheeks feel hot. I look from side to side as I cover the title with my hand. We don't know who the Oklahoma attackers are yet. If they turn out to be Muslim, I don't want the other passengers to make any assumptions about me. I close the book gingerly as I continue to listen to the broadcast.

There were airplane hijackings of course, mostly before my time. And the FLQ crisis in Montreal that defined the early seventies and about which I had done a lively presentation for my eleventh-grade social studies course. The nuclear-war fears of the mid-eighties capped by the nightmarish film *The Day After*. Those threats now feel like historical relics, things to study and perhaps be fascinated by. But something feels different now. The kind of large-scale bombings that Israelis know all too well might now prove to be a feature of life in North America. And while I had remained on guard here in Israel since that early bus attack back in

Tel Aviv back in October, always wondering in the back of my mind whether I'd be safer back home, maybe, now, I am realizing, everywhere is as safe—or as unsafe—as everywhere else. Terrorist bombings. Misogynistic violence. The sun's cancerous rays.

I look around at the other passengers. They are all wearing serious expressions: a momentarily united audience trying to piece together the circumstances of the latest reported violence, feeling a sense of odd solidarity with Americans who are normally spared this kind of thing, as the bus shoots past the fields of the lower Galilee toward the coast.

CHAPTER 10

Razors

1986

I am lying on the narrow, antique wooden bed in the room I've been given to use on Thursdays and Sundays, the days I sleep over at my dad and stepmom's house. My stepmom, who is much different from the Archie comics-collecting girlfriend my dad used to have who didn't want me to sleep over, likes when I come for dinner and sleep over. She's trying to create a family feeling between me and my dad and her and her two kids, like when she presents me with birthday cakes with pink candles as tall as rulers and as thin as blades of grass. The room I sleep in at my dad and stepmom's new house, in Vancouver, is tiny. But it's the only bedroom that has a view of the North Shore mountains. But tonight I can't see the mountains—or anything else—because my forehead is pressed into the yellow pillowcase.

I'm lying face down because lying on my cheek is painful. It's painful because I am wearing huge, square, blue metal earrings and the posts slam into my neck when I turn onto my side. But I can't remove the earrings because I'm still in the post-ear-piercing period—six weeks or so—and I've forgotten my small sleeping studs at my mom's. I got my ears pierced in Winnipeg, after camp. As we were walking to the salon, my friend Nikki and I got into an argument about what to call the shopping center next to Eaton's. I called it the mall. She called it Eaton Place. Mostly, we were both sad that I was moving away to Vancouver in a few weeks. She promised to come visit me that winter. I promised to return

© The Author(s) 2021
M. Sucharov, *Borders and Belonging: A Memoir*,
https://doi.org/10.1007/978-3-030-53732-6_10

next summer to camp. And we said we'd try to talk on the phone as often as we could. Hopefully our parents would let us, given how expensive long-distance calls are.

But nothing—the promised reunion with my Winnipeg friends or the thought of camp next summer—can help drown out the thoughts haunting me now. The pain of those metal posts is nothing compared to the flames licking my insides when I think of what lies twenty feet away from me. I'm picturing my stepmom's pink plastic Gillette razor on the edge of the bathtub. As soon as the image fades away, it flashes right back.

My heart races, and I wonder, *what if I take the razor to my wrists? I could kill myself right there.*

The words scroll through my mind. I am horrified by my thoughts. I don't *want* to kill myself, but how do I make sure that I don't? What if I lose control?

For the last few months, I've had a terrifying, unwanted obsession with suicide. I don't know when it started exactly. Maybe it was the novel I read last year, about a teenager who tries to kill himself. Maybe it was the public service film our youth group leaders showed us at the community center. And now I cannot make the images go away. Razors. Wrists. Suicide. To *commit* suicide. I try to fall asleep as the vision of the pink plastic razor on my wrists jockeys for my attention, and I lie awake, my heart pounding from the pinballs ricocheting off my insides. I feel terrorized and utterly alone.

This past summer, I had been holding my baby cousin at an outdoor restaurant in Stanley Park, with my extended family nearby. We were standing next to a balcony overlooking a steep drop-off. My mom and stepdad and grandparents and aunt and uncle were all talking at the same time, until my grandfather motioned to everyone that he wanted to speak. "Quiet, everyone," my mom said. "Zaida wants to say something." My mom's facial muscles tensed. Everyone looked from her to my zaida and back again. He didn't necessarily need my mom's help to be heard; he was healthy and robust for his age. But he hated not being listened to, and my mom couldn't bear it when he got frustrated.

"I wrote a poem," he said. "Just a minute." He retrieved a folded paper from his trousers pocket, carefully smoothed it out, and looked at us.

"Go ahead, Daddy. Everyone's listening," my mom said.

My zaida cleared his throat. "Sparkling sea, joyous sky bursting colors, trees that proudly grace the land.

Sighing leaves, a melody of an eternal song
resonance of instruments yet undiscovered."
We looked at one another.
"Very good, Daddy," my mom said.
"Yeah, Zaida, that was very nice."
"Wait. I'm not finished yet," he said, his voice rising.
"A storm —
buffeting ships at sea, lightning, and shattering thunder.
Rising sun —
heralding the dawn, blazing sunset
A full moon at horizon's edge—all of these and more!"
"Daddy, that was very good," my mom said again. We all nodded.

Usually, I was fascinated by these little family dynamic moments where my mom was playing out her own childhood again, trying to stave off her father's bursts of anger over trivial things. But that day I was having trouble focusing on the conversation. What if I dropped my baby cousin over the railing? I was terrified by my private thoughts. The words kept pounding my temples. Flames licked my insides. My baby cousin was wearing little white shorts and a red collar shirt. I hugged him tightly as I struggled to banish the horrible images from my mind.

On Monday morning, our English teacher, Mr. Baines, sits across from us wearing tight gray dress pants, a short-sleeve shirt with a wide collar, and brown dress shoes. "Tell us more Tupper stories!" comes a voice from the back row. Tupper is the high school on Vancouver's east side where Mr. Baines used to teach before moving to our school, on Oak Street. To us, the east side represents toughness, gangs, delinquency, and danger. The west side has stylish clothing boutiques and trendy hair salons.

Mr. Baines regularly tells our eighth-grade class tales about troubled youth with guns and knives and, sometimes, suicide attempts. The other students giggle loudly and sigh and gasp and call out for more, but the stories make my skin feel prickly. I can't bear discussions of troubled youth and drugs and *suicide*, that word that has been terrorizing me in the back of my mind. The word *suicide* feels contagious. I want to cover my ears, but of course I can't. Not with everyone watching.

"OK, OK, that's enough Tupper stories for today," Mr. Baines says. My shoulders relax. "This week we're starting a new writing exercise. It's called a head dump."

I look up, listening closely to the instruction to clear our desk except for a pen and two sheets of lined paper. "When I say *go*, you're going to unzip your heads"—he makes a slow, circular motion around his skull— "and dump the contents of your brain onto the page."

My curiosity has turned to fear.

As Mr. Baines gives the signal, everyone puts their head down and begins to write. But I am frozen, barely clutching my pen, palms sweaty. I do not want to dump my head and face my thoughts in writing. My thoughts are my enemy.

This is a head dump, I write. I'm stalling for time. Maybe I can fill half a page with grammatically correct sentences that reveal little. Maybe I can even practice some Hebrew rhymes, the kind we need to do at camp when we write songs and cheers. I force myself to write something. Anything.

We are sitting here in our classroom on Oak Street with fluorescent lights built into the ceiling. We are supposed to dump our heads. Head dump. Head dump. Head dump. Zippers around our heads.

I'm thinking of singers. Thompson Twins. Corey Hart. Bryan Adams. Maybe Ellen and I will go to the Corey Hart concert together. It's at the PNE. It will be my first concert. I hope it's safe. Head dump. Head dump. How much longer?

It's the best I can do. I don't want to write anything about what's actually in my head. I don't want Mr. Baines to think I'm crying out for help. I don't want to have to visit the guidance counselor's office far away from the rest of the classrooms, in the corner of the lowest floor. That's where *troubled kids* go. There are a few students even in our nicer west Vancouver school who still smoke and shoplift and take drugs; the ones who skip class, get pink slips, and have to visit the vice-principal's office. But I don't want to be anywhere near them. All I know is that I am desperate for the swirling to go away.

With a minute left in the assignment, I turn and stare out the window. Our classroom faces the same way as the tiny room at my dad's, and from here, too, I can see the mountains. I study the brown peaks—soon they will be pretty and snowcapped; for now they are hosting the autumn hikers while awaiting the winter skiiers. I stare at the shifting gray clouds, and then glance down at the track encircling the field. I'm longing for the bell to ring. But after school, I know, will only be a tiny bit better. I can distract myself with homework and TV. Maybe I'll stop off at Hill's clothing store in Kerrisdale on my way home to flip through the racks of Esprit T-shirts and Mexx sweaters. Maybe I will treat myself to a Purdy's ice cream bar. But this will only distract me a little bit, I know, because my thoughts follow me wherever I go.

That evening, I sit with my dad in his living room and let my tears fall. The old-style house, built in the 1920s, has thick gray stucco walls and a peaked roof; the living room has a brass coffee table, antique wooden end tables, and a Persian rug laid over hardwood floors.

"I'm scared and sad and I don't know why," I say. My dad gives me a blank stare.

It must be hard for him to see his daughter upset, I think to myself. He's a psychiatrist who sits in his office and listens to his patients' problems all day and now he has to come home for the evening and see his own daughter suffering.

Or maybe he's just spacing out. I get frustrated sometimes, wondering if he's listening. I know he often isn't. Often, he's in his own world. He has an "active mental life," he likes to say, when I confront him. "Dad! Did you hear what I said?"

My dad calls a psychiatrist he knows. A couple of weeks later, I sit across from her in her well-appointed Vancouver office and I don't know how to explain what's bothering me. I wish my Dad could just help me. This psychiatrist, sporting a tidy bob and a blazer, seems nice enough, but having to articulate my fears to this person seems almost as scary as the fears themselves. "Being a teenager can be hard," she says.

Over the next several weeks at school, Mr. Baines continues with the head dump exercise and I become skilled at writing what's on the margins of my mind, carefully avoiding the jagged center. In January, we begin our modern novel unit with John Steinbeck's *The Pearl*. Reading it makes my stomach swirl. There's no razors or suicide. But a sense of melancholy overtakes me as I read about the poor pearl diver, Kino, his wife Juana, their baby, Coyotito, the scorpion bite and the ocean pearl that changes their life forever. I feel mostly lonely and stomach-swirling all that year.

One thing that makes me feel a bit more cheerful is a creative project Mr. Baines assigns, which he calls a Pride Project. The twelfth graders did one for their unit on Chaucer's *Canterbury Tales*, and I like the medieval castle made of marshmallows that one student made, and the medieval theater skit performed by others who walked around that day in their costumes. One of those students is the high-schooler I have a big crush on. I've memorized his timetable and I like to watch him practice the drums in jazz band, during the early-morning period where I have to arrive early because I get a ride from my mom and stepdad's place in the suburbs with a family friend who teaches at a nearby school. Staring at him through the tiny window in the music room door eases the frightening swirls for a few minutes, at least.

For my Pride Project, I decide to try my hand at an oil painting. I rifle through my drawers and find a French beret and a smock. In the garage, I make a paint pallet and set up a makeshift easel. In between applying layers of paint, I munch on a Crispy Crunch bar from my stepdad's ready candy supply in the extra fridge.

When my mom comes into the room—the garage is attached to the office where they keep their sales invoices—she stops. "Why are you wearing that wool beret for painting? And that blouse isn't a smock." Her voice rises sharply. "You know you're not supposed to wear your *good clothes* for doing messy activities."

"Mom, I wanted to wear this. Let me do what I want!" I yell back.

"Who's going to wash them when you get paint on them?"

"I will!"

"You've never done laundry before in your life!"

"So I'll learn!"

We are both yelling now, until my mom turns and leaves. My heart is beating hard. My mom knows I've been struggling this year. She knows about my anxieties. Usually, she tries to buoy me up by being a "stage mother," as she proudly calls it when she watches, proudly, from the auditorium seat, as I sing and act in school musicals and plays. "That's my daughter," she whispered to the parent sitting next to her when I starred as King Antiochus in the Chanukah play in grade 5, beating out the boys to land the loudest and most energetic role.

I take a bite out of my Crispy Crunch, grab the paintbrush, and mix a new shade of blue.

My painting is not gallery-worthy, but it'll do.

By spring, we've moved onto a Shakespearean poetry unit. "We're going to learn iambic pentameter," Mr. Baines says. "By the end of the week, you will all be experts. I promise. Try saying *Da-DA* five times. Try it!"

I say *Da-DA* and tap out the syllables on my thigh.

Mr. Baines grins as the room fills with a cacophony of sound.

Over the next few days, I conjure up Shakespearean-style words and phrases and sentences. Soon I am writing sonnets.

A mist of love dispersed throughout the air;
the droplets fall but never do they land ...

My stepdad praises my poems and asks me to recite them at family brunches. Just as my counselor, Harry, described it, I am my family's performing seal. Two years ago, at my Bat Mitzvah, I recited my haftarah with Broadway-inflected pride, and basked in the glow of my rabbi telling the congregation how beautiful he had found my chanting. Now, I write and recite sonnets in exchange for sweet cheese kugel and spinach and red onion salad and the comfort of my aunts and uncles and cousins, as the strict meter and constrained form help me find my voice, and help me avoid the head dumps with the jagged edges and help force my horrible thoughts to the side while I pray that they wither away and die like the slugs on the sidewalks of Vancouver when you pour salt over them.

That summer I return to camp, where I am in the advanced-camp program now. My red sleeping bag feels like a private cocoon, and my cabin feels more like my home than the tiny room at my dad and stepmom's.

There on the Canadian prairie, there is no mountain view. We can't even see the lake from the main campsite. Our camp is set astride the highway, and we have to cross the busy road and walk a little ways to get to the beach. There are small trees dotting the campsite, but we mostly don't notice them because our focus is on the buildings: the *chadar ochel*, the *ulam*, the cabins. There are mosquitos and huge puddles and muddy grass. But we love camp more than anything. It's all ours.

A few months ago, my uncle on my mom's side gave me a shiny black and gold poster from the opera *Aida*, where he'd landed a part as an extra in the chorus. At my mom and stepdad's, I already had a poster that I loved: Saul Steinberg's 1976 *New Yorker* cover, a simple drawing of Manhattan in the foreground, and faraway countries, lying beyond the Hudson River and the Pacific Ocean, in the distance. So I brought the *Aida* poster to my dad's house, planning on affixing it to the wall in my new bedroom: a slightly larger room on the renovated main floor, with built-in lighting sconces on the dusty-rose walls. In an antique secretary desk, I keep a few pairs of clean underwear and socks, but I don't really keep anything else of mine here because I don't feel it's really my room. When my stepmom saw the poster, she balked. "I don't want tacks damaging the walls," she said. "We've just painted."

I stayed silent, avoiding her eyes. When she left the room, I began to cry, my stomach in knots. My dad didn't stick up for me on this issue of the poster. He was busy, in his own world. I wondered why he didn't notice my tears as I cried in my renovated bedroom that's sort of mine but not really.

Years later, my dad will sit across from me at the family cottage on a small island in British Columbia and I will tell him about this incident with the poster. He will say he doesn't remember it and he will tell me he's sorry for spacing out during those years. There was lots of stress on him, he'll say, with the high interest rates and a big house to pay off and many hours of seeing patients to service the debt, and finding a new community of colleagues in a new city. I will cry and he will cry and that will make me cry harder, and I will be torn between being glad I finally unburdened myself and wishing I hadn't said anything because seeing him cry is almost too much for me to bear.

But here, at camp, the walls feel like they are all mine. We can even write our name and all the years we've attended—in thick black felt pen. And I do.

At camp, I don't have to worry about the blank sheets of loose-leaf paper staring back at me while Mr. Baines urges us to unzip our heads. At camp, pinballs never ricochet off my insides and flames never lick my guts. At camp, my head is my muse, not my enemy: all I need to think about are the best tunes for team songs, and the best Hebrew words for team names, the most imaginative settings for themed dinners, and the best ways to impress the judges with my *ruach*. At camp, my mind never betrays me.

What we are most looking forward to this summer, now that we are fourteen, is the special evening program just for our age group that we've heard so much about over the years. It's a late-night role-play simulation called *Layl Rusiya*, or *Layl Roos* for short. Russia night.

We must pretend we are Soviet Jews trying to escape the confines of the antisemitic Communist regime. Our goal is to try to immigrate to Israel. Our counselors are KGB officials and other Soviet bureaucrats who delight in issuing a series of arbitrary and ridiculous directives as we try to navigate the intricate and frustrating web of Soviet bureaucracy. Grasping the identity papers handed to me by my counselor, I eagerly embody the role of an adult Soviet Jewish refusenik, as I try my best to banish the memory of the only adult Soviet Jew I have known in real life: Dimitri, who punched through our window when I was seven, and left spots of blood on our gray wooden stairs.

Our counselors take the opportunity to be mean and sadistic. They yell at us to get down on the ground and do push-ups. And then sit-ups. And then jumping jacks. They create endless administrative hurdles we must overcome. We feel humiliated and dehumanized. But it's all part of the game. And years ago, they tell us, the counselors were way more sadistic. Years ago, they would make everyone blow bubbles in mud puddles, and if someone had a real-life weakness, they would use it against that camper in the cruelest way. They called the diabetic campers sugar babies. In the days leading up to the program, we whisper about these stories that have been passed down to us over the years, never quite knowing if they are true or not.

As the game begins, we line up inside a small cabin. The walls have been draped with black garbage bags. Behind a desk sit three counselors. This is the bank; we need to withdraw currency for our escape. But we must not reveal our true aims to the officials.

"Bank hours are 7:31–7:54," one counselor says, using an exaggerated Russian accent. "The time is now 7:55. Come back tomorrow."

I sigh, my shoulders tensing, and look around. "Can't you make an exception just this once?"

"Do the chicken dance and sing 'Hatikvah' backwards," one of them says. "And we will consider it."

Once I get through the first station, I am allowed to advance to the next one, and the next, and the next, until night has fallen and I'm climbing a tall wooden structure, with the only illumination the borrowed light from the streetlamps dotting the highway a hundred meters away. On the top level of the structure sits an imposing counselor, his face lit from below by a flashlight. In real life, this counselor is an excellent singer and is head of the drama club. I remember that he played Tony in the Winnipeg Jewish high school's production of *West Side Story*. But tonight his official demeanor frightens me a little. This is my final interrogation. If I pass, I will be allowed to land in Israel, i.e., the *chadar ochel*, the dining hall.

"What are your intentions in leaving our country?" he asks me, his eyes steely and his voice deep.

I struggle to come up with the right answer. Is this a trick question? Should I admit to this official that I'm actually trying to leave? Does he know I'm trying to get to Israel? Does he even know that I am Jewish?

My last question is answered as he asks me, "Why do you Jews not love our country?"

"Um, we do love the country," I say, before adding, under my breath, "It's the country that doesn't love us."

"What did you say?" His voice rises.

"Nothing, comrade! God bless the USSR."

I wonder whether I've messed up again by mentioning God. Isn't the Soviet Union atheist? Now I'm confused, and I try to avoid his gaze.

After five long seconds of silence, he hands me my papers. "Run!" he says.

I climb down as quickly as I can, careful not to trip on the rungs of the ladder, and spring across the grass and gravel in my rain boots toward the *chadar ochel*. I run up the four wooden stairs, grab the metal handle, and feel the familiar weight of the doorknob in my hand. I sigh with relief as the hinges squeak.

Inside, counselors and campers have broken out in song and are dancing the hora. There are plates of kosher chocolate-and-vanilla sandwich cookies and rows of ice cream in Dixie cups. There are cartons of milk and pitchers of bug juice. I join in the dancing, my chest sweaty and my face chilled by the night.

At the end of the program, those of us who didn't make it to Israel are invited to sit alongside those who did. The staff leads us in a debriefing discussion. I remind myself that these Soviet Jews are other people, not me, and not my parents, despite my obviously Russian name.

I have never fully understood my family's connection with Russia. When my mom called Dimitri a *Russian Jew*, I took it to mean that we weren't. And I always wondered why the other Ashkenazi kids in my Jewish school—except for the two or three who actually immigrated from the USSR to Canada as children, decades after my grandparents did, before the Russian revolution—don't have as Russian a name as I do. People later tell me that they think that my paternal great-grandparents, living in Odessa, changed it to sound more Russified. Maybe they were seeking protection through assimilation. I don't really know.

"For those of you who didn't make it to Israel, how did you feel?" our counselor asks.

"Shitty. Like we were doomed. And like we were missing out on the screwball ice cream!" We all laugh, in appreciation of the reference to the little plastic cones of strawberry ice cream with a gum ball at the bottom that have become a camp tradition.

"And for those of you who made it to Israel, how did you feel?"

"It was awesome," Leah said.

"It felt like coming home," I added.

Israel, I believe with all my being, is the answer to our collective dilemma. Israel is the solution to the centuries of Jewish persecution, to our mixed-up Diaspora identity where Hebrew was neglected for so long and now lives in tender corners like in my hometown of Winnipeg and in my summer camp that is like nowhere else on earth. And while I'm gradually becoming aware of the Palestinians—their Intifada will start a few months later, thrusting the occupation into my consciousness more squarely, I am convinced of the justness of our Zionist cause, certainly in its liberal form.

Three years later, in 1989, when I'm a second-year counselor, I will argue with the head staff about this program. "Glasnost and Perestroika are now happening. Gorbachev is in power. We've got to update the program to reflect reality. We shouldn't be teaching the campers that the whole world is constantly against us. Things are changing." I will be insistent.

The head counselors—both male—will be even more insistent as they seek to humor me with a half grin. *You're cute in your earnestness*, their eyes will declare, and I will wonder why I can't manage to convey my position with more authority.

Four years after that, when I am now on head staff and am a judge for a program of television-inspired skits, I will try to convince other counselors that something they want to do is unacceptable.

"You can't paint your campers' faces with brown paint. It's wrong. That's called blackface. It's racist."

"But it's Prince of Bel-Air. This is part of the costume. There's nothing racist about it."

I glance around at the graffitied cabin. We are deadlocked, the racks of costumes in the corner absorbing the tension.

This time the counselors, who are my age, don't think I'm cute in my earnestness. Their expressions tell me I'm self-righteous and irritating. A few weeks earlier, they had teased me for using what they called a faux-Israeli accent. "We're at camp, not at the Knesset," they had said. "We say chadar ochel, not chadarrrrrr ochel." I used to say chadar ochel just like them. But I had just returned from my year in Israel and I had adopted the Israeli rolled-R.

Their gaze demands that I justify why I am trying to take the fun out of camp when our job as counselors is to write and stage plays and skits, and to design makeup and assemble props and get the costumes just right for the judges who hopefully will give us a high score and the show must go on and how else are you gonna get Ashkenazi Jewish kids to look like Will Smith?

And I will struggle as I toggle between falling into the feather-bed abyss that is camp and all its nostalgic comforts, and staying upright—and sometimes outside the circle—to keep my critical faculties sharp. Sometimes balancing between those two places will feel like walking a tightrope. Sometimes it will be lonely; often I'll wonder why I feel like the only one who yearns for these two worlds simultaneously, and sometimes, I will fall right off.

CHAPTER 11

Panic

2013

I grab the basketball that has just bounced off the rim in my attempt at a lay-up and put it between my knees so I can examine my palms. They are red and white and itchy, splotchy and swollen. I look at my arms. They are red and splotchy too. I leave the gym and walk to the bathroom. I look in the mirror. My face matches my hands.

What the hell?

I continue through the bathroom, into the locker room, and out to the lifeguard station next to the pool. I find a young woman wearing a T-shirt that says *matzil*, lifeguard, the JCC pool staff uniform. "I think I need a Benadryl," I say.

I figure I'm reacting to the cleaning solution used on the gym floors. I've seen the spray bottles in the fitness center. Lemon Quat, the hand-written label says. As a board member, I'd been pressing to get the facility to switch to green products, and I'm suspicious of this one.

"Maybe I should rinse off in the shower," I say.

"I better go with you." The lifeguard takes my elbow and leads me into a stall where I undress. My knees buckle but I feel her grip and manage to stay upright as the hot water runs over my body. She drapes me in a towel and leads me to a small sofa in the staff area next to the pool deck. My coach has joined us now, carrying my bag. He tells me they've called an ambulance.

© The Author(s) 2021

M. Sucharov, *Borders and Belonging: A Memoir*,

https://doi.org/10.1007/978-3-030-53732-6_11

I grab my phone and text my dean to cancel the meeting we have scheduled for early tomorrow morning, explaining that I'm heading to the hospital. "I'm so sorry to hear!" he writes back almost immediately. "Please take care of yourself!"

And then I call my husband, who's at home with our two kids. "I'm having some sort of allergic reaction. I don't know what time I'll be home. The lifeguards are watching me."

"OK, text me when you know more. Love you."

The paramedics arrive. They lift me onto a stretcher and I look from one to the other. "This isn't normal," one paramedic says. She injects me with something and lifts me onto a stretcher. "You know that, right?"

I nod. Normal; not normal. I'm not sure what she expects me to say. They're talking among themselves now. "*Blood pressure dropping.*"

I notice the skylights straight above—I've never looked at them from this angle—and I feel myself being wheeled out of the building—now I feel the paramedics lifting the stretcher up the five stairs between the fitness area and the lobby, into the waiting ambulance.

Soon I am in the ER at the Civic Hospital. The last time I was at the Civic was when I was in labor with my son, enjoying the numbing effects of an epidural and the sound of Neil Diamond on my iPod.

The doctors move quickly. They inject me with more needles. They stare down at me, talking quickly. I feel the jabs in my thighs. Now there's a cuff on my arm.

I don't like the pain. I protest. "Is this bothering you?" the doctor says, with an edge of confrontation. I mumble something. I exclaim with the fear of needles and my body being jabbed and prodded.

"It's probably an allergic reaction," the doctor says. "Are you allergic to anything?"

"Not that I know of," I say. "Maybe it's the cleaning solution they used on the gym floors."

The doctors look at one another uncertainly.

Eventually, they leave me alone to rest, fitting me with a clip on my finger to monitor my heart rate. Twenty minutes later, I make my way into the bathroom. Looking in the mirror, I see that my entire body is red and puffy. I make my way back to the bed and try to sleep but end up checking Facebook. I need some companionship and some sense of normalcy. At 4 a.m., the doctors hand me a prescription for an EpiPen and tell me I can go home. "You should make an appointment to see an allergist."

My husband can't leave our kids at home alone to come get me, so I walk out the front doors of the hospital to hail a taxi. It's dark and cold, and I am drowsy.

The next day, I email the head of the JCC to tell him what happened. "I wonder if it was that Lemon Quat. The stuff the maintenance staff uses to clean the floors of the gym," I say. "The splotches seemed to start on my palms, as I was bouncing the ball."

And then I think back to the events of that evening. Before playing basketball, I had sat upstairs in a small boardroom, attending a Jewish community executive meeting. And an hour before that, I'd make a quick stir fry at home: frozen shrimp, steamed rice, sautéed broccoli. Shrimp. Shrimp means shellfish, and shellfish, I know, is a common allergen. But I've eaten it all my life. Prawn tempura sushi in Vancouver, near the beach. Shrimp cocktail in Winnipeg, when I was a kid. Shrimp and scallion pancakes that we like to make for parties. Seafood spring rolls our children's caregiver and her friends prepared for Steve's fortieth. Shrimp salad rolls—wrapped in thin rice paper, along with peanut sauce for dipping—that our friends in Toronto would make us when we visited for the weekend. Shrimp shumai when we'd go for dim sum on Cambie Street in Vancouver with my in-laws. Shrimp pad thai on Wisconsin Avenue in Washington, DC, with Steve, while we were in grad school. Prawn ramen at Wagamama in London with a friend I visited during reading week at McGill. Szechuan shrimp with friends on Christmas Eve in Ottawa on Somerset Street. Shrimp skewers on our barbecue during the hot, humid Ottawa summer. Crab cakes at restaurants we couldn't afford in Washington, DC. Whole crab sprinkled with Old Bay seasoning in Baltimore at restaurants we could afford, eaten at long tables covered with butcher paper. And fresh lobster just two weeks before tonight: a feast that a friend had brought back from Nova Scotia; we ate it for lunch while our kids enjoyed an extended playdate during the teachers' strike.

By Friday, I'm at the allergist's office, where the nurse pricks me with every possible serum and I look at my arms and see hives developing where the shrimp and crab samples have entered. Now I'm scared *and* itchy.

I go to the pharmacist to get an EpiPen. And then I write about my experience in my local column for the *Ottawa Jewish Bulletin*. Because of the laws of kashrut forbidding the consumption of shellfish, it was a pyrrhic victory for the shrimp and lobster, I write. My editor later tells me that a local religious leader complained to him that my column was disrespectful. That I was honoring *treyf*. An acquaintance reads my column and emails me to suggest that one EpiPen isn't enough. You can have a rebound reaction, she writes. So I order a second.

I update my friends on Facebook. I crack more jokes about kashrut. And now I actually start to seek out kosher food. This, after I'd written a column a year earlier declaring a personal war on Jewish dietary law. It's pointless, I had argued, to follow a set of rules divorced from all ethical values—values such as health, social bonds, workers' rights, and concern for the environment. But now the hechsher, the kosher marking on packaged products, is my personal lifesaver.

Spring turns into summer. In mid-July, I am in cottage country in Ontario. My husband and I, along with our son, are picking our daughter up from camp. That evening, we go out for dinner with another family. I am still eating at non-kosher restaurants for now, as long as I instruct my servers about my allergy. Our waitress promises to bring me a safe meal.

"Do you want to taste my salmon?" the other father asks. I take a bite.

I immediately regret it. We hadn't told the kitchen to make *his* meal safe for me.

A few minutes later, my daughter examines my face. "What are those red dots, Mom?" she asks. My stomach flips.

We pay the bill and make our way to the car. I look in the passenger-side mirror and see the red dots my daughter saw. Suddenly, my body feels like it's shutting down. My stomach is swirling like it's never swirled before. I inject myself with my EpiPen. It doesn't hurt as much as I thought it would. In fact, it doesn't hurt at all. I'm frozen with fear. I instruct my husband to call 911 and turn around to face my five-year-old son in the back seat. (My daughter has decided to ride back to our hotel with the other family.) It's okay, I tell him, trying to muster a smile. "Mommy will be fine." My voice is coming out higher than usual. In his stillness, I can tell that he's trying to figure out whether he should be scared or not.

The paramedics arrive a few minutes later and load me into an ambulance. The adrenaline from the EpiPen has sped me up, and I am talking quickly. They take me to the regional hospital where the doctors examine me. "No sign of anaphylaxis," one doctor says. "You were having a panic attack."

Panic attack. I'm a bit relieved, I guess. But I'm still not altogether reassured that I won't have an actual allergic reaction in the future.

My body is loaded up with adrenaline from the EpiPen and Benadryl from the hospital and I'm drowsy and awake, all at the same time. I spend the next ten hours in bed at the inn we're staying at, sleeping fitfully.

A week later, a friend invites me and another friend for lunch. The three of us gather on her back patio at a small round table. I have told the host about my shellfish allergy. She serves us bagels and cream cheese and smoked whitefish and tossed salad. I spread some vegetable-flavored cream cheese on a bagel and bite into it. I look down at my plate and notice something pink emerging from the cream cheese. "Is that shrimp?" I ask her, my voice quivering. She shakes her head deliberately. "There's no shellfish here," she says warmly but firmly.

Now I feel a hot wave course through me. I excuse myself and go to the powder room to look in the mirror. "Shit," I say to myself, my heart pounding. I recognize this feeling all too well, though I've not had it since I was a kid and my guts started swirling when I saw a crippled person, or when I was a teen and thought about razors. It's a dirty trick. Something is terribly wrong but this is just panic but something is terribly wrong and I must do something urgently. This hot wave of anxiety tells me something is wrong though there probably isn't actually anything wrong but really there is. Something terribly wrong.

Not long after that, I am playing cards with my son in my room. My daughter is at day camp and my husband is at work. My guts start to swirl again. I touch my face. I feel a raised bump. The side of my tongue feels itchy. "We've got to go outside," I say to my son. He looks into my face, waiting for his next cue. I grab my bag and a sun hat for him and buckle his sandals and we drive down the street to my doctor's office.

"Do I look okay to you?" I ask the nurse behind the desk.

"You look fine," she says.

"You don't think I'm having an allergic reaction?"

"I don't see anything wrong." She suggests I take a walk around the building and return in a few minutes if I need to.

"We're here if you need anything. Anytime." She gives me a sympathetic look, and I blink back tears.

I take my son's hand; he has been silent this whole time. I buckle him back into his car seat and drive home.

I start to avoid eating all fish. At the fishmonger the fish lies on ice right next to the shellfish and surely the workers touch one right after lifting the other. And I decide I can't trust restaurants anymore, though I make an exception for kosher ones, and ones that are strictly vegetarian.

There aren't really any kosher restaurants in Ottawa, though. I search carefully for a hechsher symbol on packaged food.

The next time I eat cantaloupe, I notice that my mouth feels itchy. I've heard there's something called oral allergy syndrome. Maybe I have that too.

I begin to avoid eating nuts. If I have a shellfish allergy, I figure, a nut allergy may not be far behind. And some people are allergic to stone fruit so maybe I should avoid cherries. And apricots. And peaches, because I have a friend who is allergic to those.

My list of self-declared "safe" foods starts to shrink. Oatmeal with blueberries. Apples. Preferably stewed, since I've heard that some people have an allergy to raw ones. Grapefruit. Cucumbers. Grapes. Cauliflower. Broccoli. Carrots. Chicken. Eggs. Cheddar cheese. Tortilla chips. Cottage cheese.

My stepmom asks me to fly to Vancouver the next month for her seventieth birthday party. They are planning on serving their favorite food: sushi. I picture attending a party where shrimp is lurking everywhere. I picture shaking hands with people and hugging and kissing them, while shrimp could be lingering on the corners of their mouths or on the edges of the paper napkins that will be strewn all around, and I don't want to go. I am scared and anxious and hurt that my dad and stepmom are putting me in this position.

I muster up the courage to explain to my dad how I feel. I wish they already knew without my having to explain.

"I didn't realize," he says. "Of course we will make sure there is no shellfish there."

Still feeling anxious, I attend the party. My mom comes with me. They've invited her too, in a gesture of inclusiveness.

My mom enjoys seeing my dad's old friends, who she knew when they were a young couple together. She has lost weight recently and is feeling confident and social. My stepmom has asked me to write a song in honor of the occasion and I perform a jazzy ditty to an appreciative crowd. Even though there is no shrimp and the sushi chef has promised that all the surfaces were wiped down, I don't eat anything. I have two glasses of chardonnay instead.

Near the end of the night I decide to taste one of the desserts: a lemon square. I grab a knife and cut myself a thin slice. It is sweet and tangy and contains just the right amount of stickiness paired with a buttery crust. I lick my lips.

Half an hour later, I am back at my mom and stepdad's house. Suddenly my stomach is swirling and my guts feel like they're in my throat. I walk into my mom and stepdad's room. My stepdad is sleeping. He's tired these days from the effects of his diabetes. "I'm scared the knife I used to cut the lemon square might have come into contact with the sushi," I say to my mom.

"I can take you to the ER," she says. This used to be her go-to phrase, when I was growing up. She always said it without irony. In seventh grade, I had noticed a protruding bump on the inside of my wrist. What if it was cancer? As we were driving down River Road in Richmond, she had offered to take me to the ER. She was serious. I declined. I eventually learned the bump was nothing to worry about: just a ganglion. As my phobia of disabled bodies had eventually been supplanted by health anxieties, so these fears about the sudden onset of cancer were soon replaced by terrorizing thoughts about suicide. While my parents, with the help of my therapist, had supplied me with the convenient explanation of divorce as a metaphor for a severed limb to explain my disability phobia, nobody tried to explain to me why I was beset by these particular awful thoughts. By the time I was an older teenager, my acute fears had mostly receded. But then came my melanoma diagnosis, which triggered worry and a sense of isolation. And now this unwelcome shellfish allergy, and these smothering pangs of terror that I thought were a thing of the past are back. If I felt I couldn't trust myself not to lose control and kill myself as a young teen, now I feel I can't trust myself to know if I'm actually experiencing an allergic reaction or if it's just a panic attack triggered by the idea of potential anaphylaxis.

I crawl into bed with my mom and stepdad, find a spot between them, and try to make myself small. I've never once lain in bed with them. Not even when I was little. And yet I am too scared to consider the moment; I am too wound up to feel comforted; I'm too absorbed in my panic to view this physical impulse as anything more than reflex.

My heart is racing. Flames are licking my insides. Something is terribly wrong but it's just a trick and maybe I should go to the hospital to check but really it's just a trick. And I'm so tired. It's three hours ahead in Ottawa and I want to go to sleep but I'm scared and I think I should stay awake and remain vigilant.

I make my way back to my own bed in the guest room decorated with the white melamine furniture that my mom used my Bat Mitzvah money to buy. My dad was mad about that but I didn't find out that he was mad until years later.

I phone my dad and he answers on the second ring. The guests have left and he and my stepmom are cleaning up. "Dad, I'm scared. I'm scared the knife from the lemon square came into contact with the sushi. What if it did? What do I do? What should I do? What if I'm having an allergic reaction?"

His voice is calm. "There's basically no chance. No one cuts sushi with a butter knife. No one cuts sushi at all. Plus, there was no shellfish here at the party."

I'm silent.

"Focus on your breathing." He counts me through the next several breaths.

"I'm so tired; I just want to sleep. But I'm scared. I'm too scared to go to sleep." My voice cracks. "What if there was cross-contamination?"

"Focus on the breathing," he says. He counts again gently.

Soon, I fall asleep.

When I return from Vancouver, I visit my doctor. I am blinking back tears. He leans toward me and I think I detect moisture in his eyes. He looks like Tom Hanks and I am grateful for his concern. "Maybe I should see a therapist," I say.

He pulls up a website of a group of psychologists in a practice downtown. "You're gonna love the building. It's totally retro."

I look at the screen over his shoulder and we read their bios together. "This one looks nice, but he's Jewish and my dad's age and I don't want to get into daddy complex transference dynamics with him," I tell my doctor. We both laugh.

I settle on a woman about ten years my senior. She looks serious and kind and intelligent in her headshot. Her bio says she specializes in helping people to change behavior patterns. She also focuses on anxiety. I like that she has a Ph.D. She'll be able to relate to my academic anxieties—the ongoing, career-angst ones about publishing and making my mark—not only the panic-inducing ones my allergy has given rise to.

My doctor writes me a prescription for clonazepam. "This will have immediate effects," he says. "Take half a pill as needed. They're addictive, so don't take too many. Next time, we can talk about something more long-term."

I thank him, my eyes brimming with tears.

The retro building with the therapist's office is more shabby than chic. I sit on the brown sofa, under the window. She sits facing me in a chair, with a small stool propping up her feet. She has short hair and a wide smile.

"Let's talk about what you would do if you were eating something and felt a reaction," she says at our first session. "What would your response plan be?"

I shake my head back and forth. There is no way I'm willing to describe the scenario that most terrifies me.

She smiles kindly and tries another way in. "If there were a reaction, it would tap you on the shoulder, wouldn't it? You'd know. You wouldn't have to guess."

I picture this proverbial shoulder tapping and while I understand what she's trying to get at, it nevertheless fills me with dread.

I sit with my knees together and cry through most of the session. It seems easier to cry than to attend to the broader issues, whatever they are, whatever general sense of vulnerability might be undergirding my fear, magnifying it until it takes up nearly every waking thought.

The following week, I stop crying for long enough to give my therapist some fodder. We talk about my parents' divorce. We parse my relationship with my father, the way I felt when my family crumbled around me, and the way I tried to get the attention of my dad, who often seemed spaced out. I relay my worries about my career: am I publishing enough? Do I meet the approval of my colleagues? I talk about the general contours of my life more than the substance of my panic. Maybe they are related. We try to find some common themes, to bring the pieces together.

A few weeks later, I am sitting in a meeting with a colleague. We are going over spreadsheets and graphs and charts about student enrolment and retention. But I can't focus on the data. My head is spinning. I'm picturing the wrapper of the energy bar I ate half an hour earlier, as I sat on the stairs in my living room before hopping on my bike to come to campus. I had read the package. There was a hechsher. But there was also this: *May contain nuts.*

I touch my face. The inside of my cheek feels itchy. I turn to my colleague. "Do I look okay to you? Do I look normal? Do you see any swelling?"

"You look just fine to me," she says.

I break down in tears and she suggests we postpone the meeting. I go back to my office, my pulse high and my breath short. I search YouTube for the Robin Thicke single "Blurred Lines." The beat matches my rising pulse and I play it on a loop, trying to counter the buzzing in my ears as I beg my panic to flee. I think about Alan Thicke, Robin's father, who starred in *Growing Pains*, and the years I spent awash in eighties sitcoms to salve my teenage anxiety.

I pull up the lyrics and try to assess their relative misogyny, grasping at any cognitive activity that might drown my visceral panic.

I take to Facebook to tell my followers I feel guilty for listening to the song and its misogynistic lyrics, but that the beat is perfect for countering my panic attacks. In revealing my mental health challenges, I am hoping to get approval and solidarity for my performed vulnerability. Facebook "likes" will serve to assuage my anxiety, a little bit, anyway.

Thinking about Alan Thicke, I then start thinking about Kirk Cameron, who, when I was thirteen and watched him on *Growing Pains*, seemed like the most adorable guy ever, and now he's a fundamentalist right-winger, and that's disappointing of course, but at least there's still Michael J. Fox from *Family Ties*, who is an inspiration for disability awareness.

The song is only helping so much so I head outside, back into the warm summer air. "How do you manage a panic attack?" I text another friend directly, one who also suffers from anxiety.

She doesn't have any specific tips. Her anxiety is more diffuse, the kind that makes her question her value, her self-worth. She doesn't get the kind that makes her think she's going to die of anaphylaxis right then and there.

Three weeks later it's September, Rosh Hashana. The cantor conducts the main service in my synagogue, and I'm one of a few volunteers leading a smaller group, chanting the late-morning *musaf* service. I've slipped on a white kittel over my blazer and skirt. Holding a travel mug of herbal tea, I'm looking at the bima, ready to take my place in a few minutes, right after the earlier service concludes. But my heart is racing and I'm filled with adrenaline and I can't just sit here quietly waiting for my turn. I leave the sanctuary and take three speed-walk laps around the foyer. Soon I resume my position and pour my energy into the *hineini* prayer. *Here I am.*

A few weeks later, my therapist encourages me to talk to my doctor about an anti-depressant. "Should I take it, do you think?" I ask my doctor. "I don't want to take drugs if I don't have to."

My doctor looks at me with his gentle Tom Hanks eyes.

"Look, some people take meds who shouldn't, and others who should take them don't. So I think it's totally fine. And I can see you're having a hard time. Yeah, I do think it's a good idea."

I know he's not used to seeing me like this. Usually, we chat casually and amiably about what I'm currently reading. He loves to hear about my work at the university. But today, his intense eyes, leaning closer to mine than usual, tell me that I'm not myself. He is offering help and I take it. He prescribes me an SSRI and I stand in line at my neighborhood pharmacy and burst into tears as I hand them the prescription. What if I get an allergic reaction from the drug itself?

Sobbing, I ask the pharmacist if I can take the first pill in front of him. I'll feel better if he watches, I think. We make our way over to a small alcove away from the main counter. I swallow the white pill, take a swig from my water bottle, and sit down, watching him as he watches me. No reaction. I seem fine. Soon, I head home. The evenings are still long and warm.

The next night I tell my husband I'm scared to take my meds. "Your mind is playing tricks on you," he says. "That's what it does. There's nothing to worry about." He looks at me sympathetically.

"But I'm scared," I say. I take a deep breath and mange to down the tiny white tablet.

By the middle of the next year, a couple of months after I've graduated myself from therapy—we both agreed I can return if I ever want or need to—I'm feeling more myself. I have settled into a generally comfortable routine when it comes to restaurants, choosing only to go to strict vegetarian or kosher ones, where I know there will be no shellfish on the premises. The panic attacks have subsided. I get an occasional pang of anxiety, but nothing debilitating. So I ask my doctor if I can taper off the meds. He agrees, and two weeks later, I am off them completely.

But a few years later, my anxiety ratchets up again. We are planning a family trip to Hawaii for Steve's fiftieth. I'm scared to go in the water. Shrimp live in the ocean, and what if the water carries the allergen onto my skin or into my mouth? I manage to avoid the ocean nearly the whole time I'm there, taking early-morning speed walks around the promenade with my dad and spending afternoons by the pool. No shellfish there.

A month later, it is Passover. My husband's family from Vancouver is visiting us in Ottawa. I make two beautiful seders, full of singing and lively discussion. Generally I prefer to eat standing up, right out of the fridge, but for this occasion I have set a perfect table—twice—dotted with white tulips and the traditional yellow *haggadot*, the Canadian equivalent of the fabled Maxwell House haggadah.

The morning after the second seder, I am eating leftovers in the kitchen. My husband is nearby. My mother-in-law is sitting on the sofa, next to my kids. As I bite into a piece of brisket, I feel a buzzing in my cheek. I go into the bathroom. My cheek has ballooned out, hard, like a baseball. My husband gets our neighbor, a physician, to come over. "It looks like an allergic reaction," he says. I stab my thigh with my EpiPen and tell my husband to call 911.

In the ambulance they keep asking me whether I'm having any trouble breathing and I don't know how to answer that because I don't trust my body to tell me what's really happening. I don't know the answer to the question of whether I'm having trouble breathing. The dirty trick is back. I'm full of worry and dread and I'm sped up on adrenaline from the EpiPen, and maybe I should take the second EpiPen just in case—when it comes to anaphylaxis, there can be a rebound reaction, which is why I always carry two.

"Maybe we should give you something for this anxiety," one paramedic says as he puts the second EpiPen out of reach.

"Do you think I'm having an allergic reaction?"

The other paramedic says yes, he thinks I am. They take me to the ER, where I sip from a plastic cup of water and try to get my groggy self to sleep.

I'm released several hours later. I go home and sleep for ten hours.

Now I'm feeling hopeless and anxious and I'm starving. I don't know what I'm allowed to eat. I must have a new allergy, I figure, because the seder leftovers didn't contain any shellfish or any shellfish-contaminated food.

I go to the allergist again, and he doesn't find any new allergies. I'm relieved. He thinks it may have been something mechanical with the way my cheeks and saliva work. He likens it to smoke coming out of the ears of cartoon characters on *Looney Tunes*. I think I understand the example, but I'm still not sure what it has to do with me.

A few days later, I am getting ready to go to a colleague's book launch. It's early evening. My kids are home. I get out of the shower and look at my face. My guts are swirling again as I look at my right cheek. It's a little puffier than my left cheek. I am desperate to find symmetry but I can't. I call my teenage daughter into the bathroom to look into the mirror with me. She's not sure she sees anything. With my heart racing,

I am not convinced. I email my colleague an apology—the same thing happened to me the other day, I explain—and instead go to the evening walk-in clinic.

The doctor looks at me. There's no swelling, he says. He doesn't see any difference between my cheeks. And he thinks he's figured out my problem. The reason why my cheek had become like a baseball last week was that I had something called a blocked salivary gland. Nothing particularly dangerous. It happens occasionally. Nothing to worry about.

I'm sort of relieved, and appreciative of his fine detective work. And it squares with what my allergist had thought. But I also still have my fears. I am scared that this might happen again. Even though he says it's really a benign thing, this blocked salivary gland, I don't trust myself not to panic if it does happen again. And all this reminds me of the true source of my nervousness: the actual shellfish allergy that I still have, the allergy that forces me to be constantly on guard. Of course this isn't the first time I've had to be vigilant. *Chefetz chashud.* Suspicious object. That phrase was drilled into us while living in Israel the first year I was there, at Hebrew University. An abandoned backpack could contain a lethal explosive. And then there was the ever-present threat, the second year I lived there, of buses exploding. But those threats were communal; they faced all of us equally. This allergy—and the hovering threat of melanoma in the background—feels like mine alone. The allergy, the moles, these are my own body betraying no one but me. I feel targeted.

With my husband out of town, I'm sitting on the bleachers at my son's baseball game. It seems that my anxiety especially creeps up when he's away—convenient, isn't it? I'm attempting to outsmart my panicky mind, but it's hard to do with the dirty trick always in play. When I look down at my left arm, on the inside, just above the elbow, I see a faded oval patch of reddish pink. At least I think I do. A flash of heat courses through me. *What is this patch?* I feel a wave of terror. I need medical help, or at least someone to tell me I'm okay. I look over at the other end of the bench. My son's friend's mom is there. She's a doctor. A psychiatrist. I consider asking her to look at my arm, but embarrassment gets the better of me, and I focus on my breathing. On my way home, by now a little calmer but still not totally, I snap photos of my skin, trying to better investigate what I thought I saw.

Now, whenever anxiety bubbles up, I take what I call anxiety selfies: close-up photos of my face so I can examine myself for a possible reaction. In the tiny pixels, I look for dots, for blotches, for hives, for signs of swelling. I investigate the natural asymmetry between the halves of my face. Is that actual swelling, or am I always like that? I press my finger into my cheek, searching for signs.

I let those photos accumulate on the photo album on my phone. In them, I am dour, staring blankly at the camera. They are like all the "before" pictures of magazine-ad makeovers. The angles are all wrong. The lighting is terrible. I'm not doing the special headshot pose I learned from a fancy photographer video on YouTube, the day I was supposed to get a professional session done but the photographer canceled. Watching the video, I learned that you're supposed to sit at an angle and squeeze your eyes together just so, and stick your forehead straight out so that the camera catches chin definition and you look chiseled.

My husband tells me to delete the photos from my phone. "They're obsessive," he says. "They don't help."

I call my therapist and resume my sessions. She gives me cognitive behavioral exercises to do at home. In the morning, I'm to face a wall in the corner of my dining room and jot down notes on all my panicky worries. At night, I'm supposed to return to the same spot and revisit those notes, to prove to myself that nothing came of those worries. I try to do the homework dutifully. But facing the wall, I'm consumed by a fiery feeling inside my body. I feel like bugs are crawling over me.

In a fit of creative energy, I decide to take up boxing. But I have a memory of my earlier allergy attack being triggered by exercise; I recall the doctor saying this was a possibility. At the very least it happened while I was in a basketball class. So by Friday evening, when my boxing class is set to start, I am a bundle of nerves. The class is in the community center's dance studio and I look into the floor-to-ceiling mirror every few seconds to check my face. Is there a blotch? What is that itch? Do I have *hives*? As my face reddens with the exertion, my fear intensifies. I can't distinguish between exercise signs and allergy symptoms. I don't trust my own ability to read my body.

As Friday evening rolls around each week, I consider avoiding the boxing class, but my husband, on the phone, sometimes in town and not yet home from work, and sometimes traveling, pushes me to go. He doesn't like to see me like this. While I sometimes wish he would just scoop me up in his arms and hold me, I'm grateful for his prodding. "A thought is simply a thought," he says, drawing on the principles he's learned in his recent foray into mindfulness and meditation. "Don't give the thoughts more credence than they deserve."

One afternoon, I'm early to pick up my kids from Hebrew school so I decide to head to the grocery store across the street to pass the time. It's late spring and warm out, and the air conditioning is on full blast. In my short sleeves I am cold and my anxiety is buzzing as I walk past the frozen food section and spot the shrimp and I can't be sure whether the chicken in the refrigerated area is packaged in the same spot as the seafood and I try to find someone to ask whether they change their gloves between tasks but no one seems to know and I'm shivering and feeling prickles of panic and I just want to go home.

I make it out with some groceries—at least I'll have something to prepare for dinner—and stand outside the synagogue waiting for my kids to emerge. I see a friend and he asks, unremarkably, "How are you?"

"I'm pretty good," I say. All I want to do is break down in tears but that would be weird. So I manage to hold my flooding emotions in check and retrieve my kids and drive them home, adopting a cheerful demeanor as I ask them how class was.

Soon enough, I realize that if I'm going to beat this, I will need to go back on the meds. I'm reminded of the possible side effects. Weight gain, compromised sexual performance. I no longer recall whether I gained weight last time, or whether my sexuality was affected. And how much do I even care about these potential effects? At least that's what I tell myself to try to push my vanity (and physical pleasure) away in favor of my mental well-being. So I go back to taking a little white pill each morning, and eating breakfast earlier than I otherwise would so I don't get an upset stomach from the medication. I gradually gain back the weight I had recently lost, as I eventually force some distance between my brain and the fears that seek to sabotage it.

Panic. It is a wizard of threat. It is a sorcerer of terror and discomfort, using the same tools—sparkly stimulation and sensory showering—that could bask a person in pleasure and delight. If it only wanted to.

Panic. It's like being a child of divorce all over again as I try to pull the pieces together: safety and danger, reality and fear, swinging between houses with different carpets, between marriages and separations, between my real home and my dad's home and the home-away-from-home that is summer camp, between the reality of the present and my nostalgia for the past, between Israel as a lived reality and my image of the place, between political poles, between parts of my community and between my community and that of others—as I try to locate a single, coherent, authentic narrative that is safe and secure and true.

CHAPTER 12

Tents

1987

It's July 1987, I'm fifteen, and the loonie single-dollar coin has just been issued by the Canadian Mint. "Is it actually called a loonie?" I say. I'm visiting the boys cabin and looking at the guys sprawled over their bunks.

"Yeah, totally. It's hilarious, isn't it?" Jason and I look at each other and laugh.

"I can't believe that prim-and-proper Canada built a nickname right into the official name of legal tender."

But we won't see the coin in real life for a while because we're away from commerce and coins and banks and bricks, for six whole weeks. We are finally counselors-in-training.

In the orange canvas tent on our overnight, the prairie sun is beating in and I'm getting hot while trying to sweep the dirt and sand away from my pillow. But I don't want to leave the spot I'm in just yet. I'm lying on my red sleeping bag, close to Jason, writing a letter home to a friend in Vancouver, while privately willing Jason to kiss me.

He has curly brown hair and brown eyes that twinkle when he cracks a joke. We've been close friends since fourth grade, when I moved to the Jewish school in the north end, from my old Jewish school in the south end. With Ron's kids joining our household, my mom and Ron had decided to move to a cheaper neighborhood so we could get *more for our money*. Our new house had gray shag carpet and a sunken family room and an orange-carpeted basement rec-room with wood-paneled walls, and

© The Author(s) 2021
M. Sucharov, *Borders and Belonging: A Memoir*,
https://doi.org/10.1007/978-3-030-53732-6_12

a real working pinball machine that the old owners had left behind and which took pennies as payment.

In fifth grade, Jason wore navy rugby pants and a red knitted kippa with little yellow Pac-Mans on it, and he had a ready supply of Paper Mate erasable pens. Our Hebrew teacher—the same teacher my dad had when he was in elementary school, and whose past, in Europe, during the war, we never asked about—called Jason's kippa *technicolor*. That always made us laugh. Five years later, Jason and I still try to crack each other up by saying "technicolor" in our teacher's thick European Jewish accent. Sometimes I worry that Jason no longer thinks it's as funny as I do, that he lives more in the present while I'm more inclined to infuse my present with the past.

The summer after fifth grade, at camp, Jason and I and another boy from his cabin would stop off at the outdoor sinks every afternoon on our way back from free swim. Jason would supply the shampoo, Body on Tap. It smelled of beer and made me feel grown-up as I bent over the row of sinks and rinsed bits of sand and seaweed out of my hair, splashing him for effect.

Now, four summers later, Jason no longer invites me to shampoo our hair together. And in the tent we share with a few others, he doesn't kiss me. But he does grab the letter I'm writing.

I make a half-hearted attempt to grab it back, but soon Jason has taken hold of my pen too. "Hi Judith," he writes, "it's Jason, Mira's friend. We are sitting here in the tent on our overnight and I've stolen her letter so I can say hi. How are you? What's new? I better give Mira her letter back before she kills me."

I appreciate the gesture but would prefer that he kiss me. Or at least invite me to shampoo our hair together.

Since the Escape from Russia program was so popular with our cohort the year before, our counselors have created a new program for us: Escape from the Holocaust. We can't wait for it to start.

After dinner, my counselor hands me a piece of paper containing a name, age, and identity. "Your wedding will take place in half an hour in the *ulam*," my paper says.

Thirty minutes later, I make my way in bridal costume to the *ulam Ben-Tzvi*, the program hall named for Israel's second president. I take my place next to the groom under a bedsheet-constructed chuppah. A counselor dressed as a rabbi stands before us.

My groom holds out a dime-store ring. "*Hinei at mekudeshet li*," he says, reading from a script. You are consecrated unto me. Then he stomps on a Styrofoam cup. Our fellow CIT's break into song and we are swept up in circles of hora dancing. Suddenly, we hear yelling as the door opens and five counselors storm the auditorium, overturning chairs and hurling curses at us.

The game has begun.

Just as in Escape from Russia, our goal tonight is to reach the dining hall—Palestine—and avoid our alternate fate: deportation to a concentration camp.

As the simulation winds down, our counselors gather us into the *moadon*, the staff lounge, the perimeter lined with candles. They distribute worksheets to complete, with titles like "Why Did the Nazis Come to Power in Germany?" and "What is the Best Form of Resistance?" and "Life in Extremis: Moral Action Inside the Camps." We are invited to consider what we would have done in these harrowing situations.

By now, compared to when I visited Yad Vashem in Israel when I was ten, I am not only immersed in the feeling of Jewish suffering, I am also trying to search for meaning beyond it. My thoughts turn to the concentration camp guards. Were they evil, I wonder? Or were they the victims of their own awful leaders? I grab a pencil and a yellow sheet of construction paper, and I begin to write.

Why am I here? I didn't do anything to deserve this. Yet, I am as much to blame for the deaths of millions as anyone else, even Hitler. I don't want to be here—stamped with a label saying "the enemy."

I am a human, no better nor worse than any prisoner here. Only my hair and eye color distinguish me from them.

There, in the distance, I can see an officer beating a prisoner. Yet, I cannot interfere—now or at any other time, for my fate is at stake as much as anyone else's.

I am one in an army of hundreds, yet I stand alone. The gun in my hand, the uniform upon my unbeaten back, were placed there by someone else's hand. They are merely symbols of false superiority which separate me from others.

Quickly, a wall is forming. It will separate us from them forever. Stop it, stop it!

(Kneels down.)

"Stop! Jew!"

I add some illustration—barbed wire and cabin barracks—before searing the paper's edges with the lit candles, for effect.

Years later, I come across the monologue in my photo album. Reading it over, I cringe at my attempt to have focused my energies that night on inhabiting the mind of the concentration camp guard. While drilling into the mind of a perpetrator is a fascinating undertaking, maybe it would have been more moral to have reflected on the experiences of my own people: the Jewish victims and survivors.

I didn't always adopt that sort of scrubbed-down universalism. There had been times when I worked hard to try to ensure that the Jewish experience of persecution and genocide was not forgotten. In twelfth grade, I had sought out the Vancouver Holocaust society. I attended their annual conference, and forged links with one of the local history professors who specialized in Holocaust education. Inspired by these scholars and activists, I took it upon myself to try to lobby the provincial government to make Holocaust education mandatory in high schools. I was shocked by the idea that some students in my province could graduate without having learned about the genocide of the Jews. I typed out documents and prepared files.

One afternoon, I approached my own high school history teacher for support. Though he didn't often discuss it, I knew from my mom—who remembered him growing up—that he was Jewish too. Walking up to his desk clutching a manila file, I asked, "Would you consider lending your support to my initiative?" I'm trying to get the provincial government to make Holocaust education mandatory, and I could really use the backing of an actual teacher."

"Uh, probably not," he said, shuffling papers on his desk and looking away. "Politics isn't really my thing." He smiled uncomfortably.

I managed a thin smile. "Thanks anyway."

It occurred to me that as much as it seemed natural that Jews would want to help preserve the memory of our people's most painful historical trauma, there were layers of self-interest at play for everyone. Maybe he feared political blowback; maybe he feared for his job; maybe the outlay that would be required of him—letters, follow-up calls—was simply too much in a demanding work schedule. And that maybe I was being fuelled by the feeling of being a teenager getting important things done, by the feeling that I would eventually get accolades for jumping through hoops that I had placed strategically high.

Before he left this earth, my father-in-law, a survivor of Auschwitz, asked his family and the many students he spoke to in high schools around Vancouver to focus on small acts of kindness, from wherever they might come. He often told a story of a concentration camp guard who, one day, offered him a bicycle to help give his legs a rest on a long march. And he told of another guard who was gentle to him one afternoon, even offering a quick smile, during the otherwise brutal factory work detail. More than anything, my father-in-law wanted people to live their lives trying to notice and offer acts of compassion. I don't know whether to regret my teenage monologue for being overly sympathetic to the Other, or to see it as a crucial chain in the link of empathy so needed in our world.

As the summer wears on, I forget wanting Jason to kiss me. Now my counselor, Mark, has a hold over me that I cannot shake. Mark is handsome, with curly hair and an angular chin. He is funny and smart and talented and confident. He sings and plays guitar and acts and draws. His Hebrew is among the best of the staff.

One night, a few of us are sitting in the costume cabin. Mark is strumming his guitar, and we are singing Cat Stevens songs and songs by the Israeli folk star David Broza. Enjoying the feel of the sofa upholstery underneath me, I am trying out my best harmonies. I lock eyes with Mark. He meets my gaze, and I'm filled with a longing that surprises me in its intensity. But he is considerably older than me, and I am self-aware enough to know that what I feel is infatuation. Still, I am enmeshed in it.

On the last day of camp, Mark lifts me up and poses for a picture. I'm wearing a khaki Cotton Ginny sweatshirt and my Israeli army pants, and my face is streaked with tears. Mark, on his way to Israel for the year, promises to write to me. When I get back to Vancouver, I hang that picture in my locker.

After camp that summer I check my mailbox every day after school, my heart beating quickly, to see if there's a new letter from Mark. His neat and even handwriting charms me. I devour his descriptions of Israeli life. I picture him sitting at a cafe on Dizengoff street, or walking along the boardwalk, or hiking in the north.

I comb his prose for crumbs of affection. "It was amazing being your counselor," he writes. "You were so young and impressionable."

Impressionable. I want it to mean that I made an excellent impression on him. But deep down I know what it really means. In my eagerness to interpret any attention as affirmation, I decide to take what isn't really a compliment as one anyway.

I count the days between missives, folding and unfolding the letters and re-reading them in the meantime, keeping a careful tally of letters sent and received. Blue ink for sent and red for received. I'm careful not to write two letters in a row, lest I seem desperate.

In his next letter, Mark includes a black-and-white headshot; he's been hoping to break into theater there. "The Israelis think they've got a real Canadian actor on their hands," he writes. I stare at the photo until I can't stare at it any more. I tuck it into my schoolbag and the next day add it to my locker, underneath the picture of us posing on the last day of camp.

Eventually, Mark begins dating someone, he tells me, an Israeli woman with a poetic name, and the letters stop coming. Eight years later, I will meet this Israeli woman by chance, through common friends, at a party in Tel Aviv. She and Mark have since broken up. "Do you like redheads?" she asks. She offers to set me up with her brother. "It's the least I can do," she says, with a laugh. I agree to go on a date with her brother, who wears a leather jacket and does tai chi and is a vegan, and we drive to the beach and he reaches for my hand in the car and I let him hold it, but I feel no stirrings of longing or infatuation or anything else.

The next summer, my friends and I are finally counselors. I arrange my room with a sheet for the door, carefully making my bed with old green sheets left over from my house with the brown carpet. Then I plug in my portable Toshiba stereo and line up my cassettes: Arik Einstein, Shlomo Artzi, R.E.M., Cat Stevens, James Taylor, and Paul Simon. I make two tall piles of oversized sweatshirts—Beaver Canoe, Benetton, Naf Naf, my blue counselor-in-training sweatshirt featuring a silkscreen of Marty McFly from *Back to the Future*, and my very own staff sweatshirt.

Reaching into my stash of chocolate rosebuds that I bought with Leah at Grant Park Plaza before camp started and that I've stored under my bed, I fall onto my sleeping bag and turn to the wall. Through layers of graffiti, I can make out various names of counselors before me. And then I spot my dad's name, written in black felt pen, in all caps: *MAX SUCHAROV, 1953, 1954, 1956,...* up to 1967. 1955 is missing from his list. That must be the year his parents didn't let him attend.

"They said it was punishment for poor behavior," my dad told me. "But I think they were short on money that year and were too ashamed to tell me the truth." The next summer he used his Bar Mitzvah gift money to pay his own way.

I grab a black marker and add my name just below his. *Mira Sucharov (Max's daughter), 81, 82, 83, 84, 85, 86, 87, 88, 89.* Then I snap a photo of the wall.

A year later, I make my bed in the same residence hall that my dad lived in at McGill. No graffiti allowed there, of course. But I think of the white cinderblock walls as storing memories and conversations. He lived on the fourth floor of McConnell Hall, at the top of the hill; my room is on the third.

By now, Jason and I have a tacit agreement to just be friends. He is busy with other relationships and sometimes I am too. I become his confidante. "She's crazy not to like you," I say, trying to salve his hurt after one girlfriend has broken up with him. I look him in the eye and try to hold his gaze. If I can be the one to make him feel better, then I will be indispensable. I want to matter. Even though we are *just friends*, it's his cabin I like visiting late at night, once the campers have fallen asleep, and it's his arms I like being held by when, on the last night of camp, wearing our blue-and-red plaid lumberjackets, we sit on the dock together, waiting for sunrise.

"This is great," he says.

I give his arms a squeeze.

One night, the director summons the staff. When we arrive, clustered in the dining hall around the center tables, his expression is serious.

"I just got a call from the city," he says slowly. "There's been a terrorist attack. On a bus. In Israel."

My muscles tense.

"Fern Rykiss," he continues, his voice cracking, "was killed."

I try to absorb the news as some of the counselors around me dissolve into tears.

All of us knew Fern.

Fern was a twelfth-grader at the Winnipeg Jewish high school. She had been traveling with a friend in Israel, just after the school's year-end organized trip to the country had wrapped up.

The director continues. "I need you to keep all your radios off for the next forty-eight hours. And hide whatever newspapers are around. We don't want the campers to find this out from us. Their parents will tell them, if they want to, when the kids get home."

Newspapers are in easy reach this week because we've been stockpiling them for the evening program involving silly gym games. We will have to rearrange.

We walk back to our cabins in silence.

I later learn that Fern was riding Bus 405 when a Palestinian militant forced an Egged bus off a cliff between Tel Aviv and Jerusalem, killing sixteen civilians. I feel my skin prickle as I picture Fern's bus lying at the bottom of the Jerusalem hills, crashed and charred.

Once the campers are in bed, I head to the flagpole, where we usually gather each night to sit and trade jokes, avoiding sleep as long as we can. But that night the mood is somber.

I find a spot on the grass among my fellow counselors. Everyone is talking quietly in twos and threes, some wiping tears away with the back of their hand. I'd moved from Winnipeg to Vancouver after sixth grade, so I didn't know Fern as well as the others did, and I'm trying to find my way in.

It's part of a phenomenon that historian Laura Levitt has traced in her writings on American Jews struggling to find evidence that they were touched by the Holocaust. "Many of them," Levitt writes in her book *American Jewish Loss After the Holocaust*, "are desperate to see themselves as part of an acknowledged history." For Levitt, that is "only part of the story. It is not so much that I want to place myself in this. .. authorized narrative," Levitt writes. "... it is that I want a place for my own stories of loss."

Fern had appeared in a dream I'd had three years earlier, not long before I moved away from Winnipeg. In the dream, we were at the YMHA where, in real life, I would spend every Saturday afternoon with dozens of other Jewish youth from all over the city. In the dream, Fern was aiming a basketball at the net when a teenage boy we knew came up behind her, stole the ball, took a shot, and missed. I tried to stick up for

her by taunting him, calling him by his last name, emphasizing the conso-
nant blend for effect. Then I was reprimanded by the YMHA director and
woke up feeling ashamed.

Over two decades later, when Gilad Shalit, the Israeli soldier held
captive by Hamas, is released in a prisoner exchange, much of the Jewish
world will celebrate, and I will write an op-ed in *Haaretz* marking the
occasion, urging Israel to take the opportunity to press for full peace.
And nearly a decade after that, I will learn that Fern's killer was among
the prisoners set free.

And then I will think about that dream, recorded in a brown Duo-
Tang on my bookshelves, part of a school project I'd completed in sixth
grade. And I will think of a photo of Fern that remains in one of my
albums. In the photo, we are standing on the stage at the Y, clapping and
singing. She is wearing red pants, a white blouse, and striped leg warmers.
She is smiling, with long brown hair and piercing brown eyes.

Right after camp, I spend a week with my friend Nikki at her family
cottage down the road before I have to return to Vancouver. Nikki and I
spend the days lounging barefoot on the grass, looking for people we
know walking along the grid-pattern streets of what feels like a little
Jewish shtetl, and eating mini-bagels with cream cheese and watching
Mr. Mom on VHS.

One night, Nikki's older cousin says he has a really cool movie to show
us. He pops a videotape into the VCR and animated grown-ups sway
and writhe to the music. "Isn't this so fucking awesome?" he says, a grin
emerging under his mustache. I am glued to the screen, my eyes wide,
staring at this movie he tells us is called *Heavy Metal*, too embarrassed to
really watch and too embarrassed to look away.

The next night, Nikki and I stroll along the boardwalk, gorging
ourselves on soft-serve ice cream and french fries. Afterward, we find a
spot to perch on a grassy hill overlooking the lake. "So many men, so little
time," I say to Nikki. We collapse into a fit of laughter. I don't really know
what I intend by the phrase. I just know I am yearning for something.
Maybe love, maybe romance, maybe admiration, or maybe just approval.
I miss camp and the songs and the programs and the counselors who
make up a world where we're always watching and always being seen.

CHAPTER 13

My Wadi

2016

Matt is a Jewish colleague who lives far away and who I've been chatting with on Facebook. Our discussions have become long and intense. "Will you be my work husband?" I ask one afternoon. It's a term I sometimes use to describe my writing or other professional partners: colleagues who help keep me grounded and connected in a profession that can feel isolating.

"Darlin', I'll be anything you want me to be."

I can't seem to pull myself away from the attention and the admiration I get from these e-chats. The conversations soon start to consume me. If Matt's words appear in my chat window, I feel alive; if they disappear, I feel depleted. I realize I've mostly lost my appetite. Soon my clothes don't fit. And then I discover I have lost over twenty pounds. Friends and acquaintances comment on my thin frame. Some compliment me. Others look concerned. "Just revved up," I say.

But despite our common ground—Jewish life, parenting, teaching, and academia in general—Matt and I have plenty to disagree about. One night, as I am telling Matt about Jabir, the Arab boyfriend I had for a few months at the end of undergrad, and he is telling me about an Israeli girlfriend he once had, and I ask, with great curiosity, whether they argued in English or Hebrew, the conversation shifts to BDS: boycott, divestment, and sanctions against Israel. I mention that I'm part of an academic group seeking to fight against the occupation *and* fight against academic

© The Author(s) 2021
M. Sucharov, *Borders and Belonging: A Memoir*,
https://doi.org/10.1007/978-3-030-53732-6_13

boycotts. I was recruited to that group through the board of a Labor Zionist group I am part of.

"Fighting against BDS? What the fuck? You're the enemy!" he writes.

A cold chill comes over me, soon replaced by a wave of anxiety. *Don't leave*, I think.

"What do you mean?" I write, trying to slow my accelerating heartbeat. "How can I be the enemy?"

"You're helping an organization that is fighting BDS."

"But we're also fighting the occupation! It's not like we're those right-wing groups." I name one of them. "We're progressive. We're the good guys here!"

"But BDS is the only thing that has a chance in hell of working. Of bringing an end to the fucking occupation and Israel's racist regime. To stand in the way of that is reprehensible."

"But that's where the money is," I say. "Jewish funders want anti-BDS initiatives. And that kind of funding helps us do other good things."

"Of *course* that's where the money is. That's no fucking excuse."

I wait a moment.

"Look, I better go to sleep," he says.

"Yeah, that's probably wise. Well, have a good night."

I log off with a pit in my stomach.

For several weeks, I fear that Matt is judging my every move on Facebook—articles I share, petitions I sign, op-eds I write, comments I make. I fear that if I don't exhibit perfectly calibrated politics, he will pull away.

At a conference not long after, I approach an Israeli friend. He's liberal, and he doesn't like the occupation either. "What do you think about BDS?" I ask.

"What do I think about BDS?" He pauses for a moment, leaning back in his chair. "It's understandable. I don't personally agree with it, but maybe if I were in the US, maybe if I didn't live in Israel, I would do it. I mean, the Palestinians have to have *some* way of protesting."

I know that I'm not posing the question entirely in the spirit of intellectual and political exploration. It's motivated by wanting to bridge my worlds, and I feel a bit ashamed of my desperation. I want everyone I respect—or at least everyone who lavishes me with attention and approval until they withdraw it—to agree. That way I won't feel like a plastic grocery bag being buffeted by the wind, like the child who went from the house with the green carpet to the apartment with the blue carpet to the house with the brown carpet.

Soon I step down from the board of the organization—the one that led Matt to call me the enemy. I am grasping for legitimacy. Whether by my own moral compass or to please those who seem to judge me most harshly at the same time as doling out affirmation in selective ways, I decide I will no longer be part of organizations that actively oppose BDS. (Neither will I join organizations that actively promote it.) It's a new golden mean for me, one that will no doubt appear too far left in the eyes of some, and too far right in the eyes of others. But I decide that I can inhabit this space comfortably enough. For now, at least.

Over the next few weeks, whenever I log onto Facebook, I glance to the right of my newsfeed to see if there is a green dot next to Matt's name, signaling that he is online. At first, not seeing the dot brings disappointment while seeing the dot brings a rush of excitement. But when my attempts at conversation go unanswered, the dot brings a jolt of discomfort and anxiety. *Why hasn't he responded?*

Eventually, I drag the Facebook window rightward with my cursor, so that the column is hidden entirely. I realize that Matt is no longer judging my posts or my politics. He is no longer paying any attention at all.

I begin to try to escape from this cycle of attention seeking and disappointment by taking long bike rides. Along the canal. Along the river. As far as the bike path leads me before it becomes a highway. I enjoy the wind in my face and the heat and the speed. I follow the curving roads that snake by Parliament and continue past pretty river beaches filled with driftwood and craggy rocks, framed by tiny purple wildflowers. But I'm not really escaping because every few miles I stop and take a photo of the view that I'll post on Facebook. The angles are artful, I tell myself. And then I take a selfie. And another, and another. Straight ahead, with the water behind me. Or from above, as I lie on a grassy patch, my bike-gloved hand perched atop my head so it's visible in the frame, and my sunglasses protecting me from the glare but really adding a bit of glamor, I hope.

And then, when I take up boxing, an idea that seemingly comes out of nowhere one night, and I find a local class in a community center and then find a proper gym with a ring and mats and heavy bags and a bell, I am equally hungry for the social media affirmation that brings. Photos, pithy posts, whatever it takes to get my colleagues to know I'm not just brains—if they even ever thought that in the first place. Maybe, if I'm perceived as being *well-rounded*, my hard-edged opinions on justice in Israel-Palestine will be perceived as thoughtful rather than reactive, as illuminating, like the meaning of my Hebrew name—*Meira*, rather than as heat for the sake of generating sparks of attention.

All these were lessons I'd later apply to writing a book on the topic of social media engagement and op-ed writing. I was supposed to be an expert helping others navigate the choppy waters, but all too often, I felt like I was drowning.

Occasionally that drowning feeling extends to my classroom. One semester in particular I felt untethered. A group of students always sat together at the back, whispering to one another and snickering throughout the lesson. I had gauged early on that some of these students were campus activists on a range of issues, including Palestine solidarity.

One day, a student raised her hand and asked about the word I had been dreading: apartheid. I knew it was my role to help students examine the political dynamics of the Israeli-Palestinian relationship. But as the discourse had become more polarized, I hadn't yet found a comfortable rhythm. I feared I would tacitly be assigned the role of debater, rather than my intended role as an educator shepherding my students through the issues.

"Apartheid," I said, with a sigh. "OK, let's unpack it." I turned to my computer keyboard. There was no blackboard in this room, so I had to type notes as we talked. It was an awkward feeling, standing with my fingertips stretched downward. I much preferred a blackboard that allowed me to turn away from the class from time to time. To breathe and gather my thoughts.

"To address the question of whether Israel is an apartheid state," I began, "let's start by asking what territory we're examining: inside the Green Line, or inside the West Bank?"

A student raised her hand. She leaned forward as she spoke. "No offense, but that's what a pro-Israel, *hasbara* person would say." I swallowed hard. "They'd try to say there is a difference between the West Bank and Israel proper." She used air quotes around "proper." "But we all know there really isn't any difference. Israel governs the whole thing. So trying to separate them out is just another way of making Israel look better than it is."

Pro-Israel hasbara person. The words ricocheted off the wall and landed with a sharp thud.

I should've taken the challenge sportingly. I should have spent a few minutes exploring the political implications of analyzing the geographic pieces separately or together. I should've taken her cue to talk about what might be at stake in each framing. Or I should have flipped it back to the class to discuss: what constitutes good framing and what constitutes loaded framing? How do we know? But I didn't do any of that. Instead, I argued.

"It's essential to distinguish between the two areas because the laws and politics of each are different," I said. My voice was rising. I was insistent now.

I could see I'd lost my audience. The group at the back was whispering. Giggling. Rolling their eyes.

Now I jumped up to perch on the edge of the desk, facing the class, my legs dangling. I lowered my voice almost to a whisper. "It's essential to differentiate between Israel and the West Bank. It's essential to understand the differences there." But my voice rose again. "We need to understand the differences if we ever want to do *something* about the fucked-up situation over there!"

The swearing wasn't accidental. I hoped to inject a little cultivated drama into the situation as a way to defuse the tension. When my daughter was a baby, whenever she'd take a minor tumble, I'd scoop her up in my arms as she cried and carry her outside, hugging her tightly and singing to her. With the Ottawa winter chill startling our faces, she would stop crying almost as soon as she had started. But the swearing didn't have the paradoxical calming effect I'd hoped for. The students continued debating me, and I ended up feeling defensive. As the term came to a close, I nursed a feeling of defeat.

After the winter break, I blogged about the incident on my university's pedagogy website where I was a regular blogger. I knew the topic might be sensitive, so I cleared the piece with my chair first. In it, I wrote:

There's a fine balance between embracing critical inquiry and pressing an activist agenda. Near the end of the term, this tension seemed to come to a head, particularly around the question of whether Israel is an apartheid state. I don't usually introduce the term apartheid in the context of Israel— I find its use more polarizing than analytically illuminating—but since it was raised by students in class, I agreed to broach it. I suggested we begin to assess the question of whether Israel is—or isn't—an apartheid state by looking at the difference between Israel's rule in the West Bank and Israeli rule within its pre-1967 borders. Rather than respond to the question, some students challenged the framing. I felt cornered. As a professor, I don't see my role as advocating for any one side or for burnishing the image of any country or government; I'm in the classroom to model how to assess claims, see where the data takes us, and generate knowledge.

I left class that day feeling uneasy.

After consulting with colleagues, the following week I opened the class session with a discussion of my hopes for the course—that we would join each other on a path of analytical engagement and open-mindedness; that we would join on a learning journey together. As I spoke, slowly and deliberately, perched on the desk in a faux-casual manner that concealed my nervousness, I feared that my message would be misinterpreted to suggest that certain political assessments are off-limits. I used terms like critical thinking and cognitive closure; paths and roads and bricolage of evidence and open minds. I don't know whether my message penetrated. I do know that the air was thick with tension. I hope my students left with something to think about. I know I did.

The next day, the Carleton teaching blog coordinator alerted me to a comment that had been posted under my blogpost. I was defensive, the student wrote. Clearly, I wasn't willing to engage at the very moment that students were trying to engage with me. I had fallen short in my role as educator. I had disappointed them.

It was all too much for me to cope with.

I took refuge in my colleagues, speaking rapidly and urgently to whomever would listen. I wanted solidarity and understanding and validation. My colleagues offered it. They shared their own struggles. They expressed admiration for my taking on such difficult subject matter. I was even invited by the teaching center to give a workshop to my peers on how to teach controversial issues. But I was still raw. I feared breaking down in tears in the workshop. So, in a rare move, I declined the invitation.

As I was about to go to an important committee meeting with the provost one evening, my teaching evaluations arrived in my inbox. I clicked on them and looked at the scores. They were by far the lowest I had received in a decade and a half of teaching. And then I read the accompanying comments and broke down in heaving sobs. That day I discovered stomach muscles I did not know I had.

I searched for the number of the provost's office. "I'll need to be on speaker phone for the meeting," I told his secretary, sheepishly. "I'm not feeling well."

As the next meeting was about to begin the following week, I was preparing a cup of tea in the office kitchen when the provost walked in. "I hope you're feeling better," he said, with a kind smile.

"It's not contagious," I said.

I knew I had to make a change in my teaching approach. Being scared of my students wasn't going to fly. I knew I needed to find better ways to address uncomfortable issues head-on. Improvising during those moments of tension clearly wasn't working.

A year or so later, an editor approached me about publishing a book on Israel-Palestine. I asked a colleague at another university to co-edit it. We brainstormed and came up with a volume for use in university classrooms that would address the most sensitive topics in teaching Israeli-Palestinian relations. We assembled twenty-two authors to discuss and debate eight of the most contentious issues in the Israeli-Palestinian dynamic from multiple perspectives. This time, I wouldn't be scared of my students bringing up the "A" word. I would bring it up first. Along with every other hot-button word. In the meantime, the following semester I deliberately invited students to make arguments for and against the applicability of the apartheid label. I emphasized that a student didn't need to agree with a given position; they just had to articulate it. And sure enough, one student, whose personal views had become clear by then, actually picked the opposing side to argue. I considered it a small victory.

When the books arrived two years later, I removed them from their packaging and stacked them on my coffee table, next to my grandmother's mid-century glass ashtray, above my McGill yearbook, and above my copies of Art Spiegelman's *Maus* and Joe Sacco's *Palestine*. I was proud of the small antidote to my personal teaching struggles that I'd helped craft in our very own laboratory. A remedy for the polarization that had sucked me into its vortex and from which I was too fragile to escape on my own.

An old schoolmate has given me a black-and-white snapshot from his family's collection. The picture shows my dad at camp, the same one I went to. My dad, wearing a dark cardigan and white slacks, was a counselor then. In the photo, he is standing behind my friend's uncle, a camper. My dad's hand is on the boy's shoulder.

I stare at the photograph for a long time. There's the familiar center field, what we called the *shetach*—the word for territory—where I used to toss a football with the guys in the waning Friday evening light. There are the white cabins: boys on one side, girls on the other. The molecules of air I imagine I can see, molecules carrying the strains of the *ram kol*, the loudspeaker, and the sounds of campers sitting at long tables in the *chadar ochel* singing the camp songs we both knew. My dad, not yet married, maybe not yet ever having kissed a girl. There is my dad enjoying the camp he always told me brought out his best self. But when I ask him from time to time to reminisce with me, he often demurs, "It's in the past."

I think about my dad now with his white beard, divorced from my mom and remarried, a psychiatrist-psychotherapist who swims laps and takes speed walks to beat his sciatica, and who has had quadruple bypass surgery, and from whom I continue to make emotional demands and who answers my calls during anxiety crises to help talk me through them. My dad, who phones me with updates about his ailing brother, my uncle. In my dad's voice I can hear his thoughts about his own mortality: bracing, aware, resigned, and sad. My dad, who explains to me now that had he the chance to do things over again, he would have considered more options when he took the paternity test and realized that my mom's baby, my half brother who was given up for adoption, was not his own. He was immature then, he says, a young man filled with fear and shame.

One of my dad's mentors during his time at camp was Uri: a brilliant, creative, and eccentric camp director. Years later, he would become one of my professors, and I reveled in the camp connection. Years after that, after a series of pointed debates over Israel, Uri would block me on Facebook. "She thinks I'm irritating," Uri told my dad after I sent him to inquire. "And I think she's arrogant."

He wasn't wrong.

Now, when a Facebook debate goes awry, I no longer send my dad to help me figure it out: there are too many of them. The subject of Israel-Palestine looms large, and among my friends and followers, there always seems to be much to disagree about. I try to keep a thick skin, but it isn't easy, and sometimes I fail miserably. If my dad does have an urge to come to my defense now, I try to dissuade him. He's a psychotherapist trained to express empathy and examine multiple sides of an issue. From him, I learned to embrace open-mindedness and to be suspicious of dogma. But social media is, all too often, a sea filled with stinging fish and sharp coral awaiting any misstep.

One recent summer, my dad happened to be visiting me in Ottawa when my social media feed exploded. After a heated debate on Twitter and Facebook stemming from an op-ed I had published in *Haaretz*, an organization on Twitter called my posts racist. I crumpled. Watching me debate my interlocutors over three days, my dad received a crash course in white privilege, racial erasure, and tone policing, and I got a lesson on the limits of my own emotional resilience. And then he got hit by the falling shrapnel. "You need a course in Racism 101," one activist responded when my dad tried to stress the importance, as he saw it, of empathy and listening. "We told you you'd get shredded," Steve said. My dad emitted a wry, sardonic guffaw. "*Racism 101!* My God. You're right. I guess they didn't want to hear my take about striving to be a good person."

Sometimes the social media stings are sonorous, shaming attacks, and sometimes the stings are silent ones. The loud attacks are public and embarrassing. But the silent kind—the ones that don't entail public call-outs but instead involve bouts of private judging—are difficult to bear in a different way. Those kind make me feel not that I've done something terrible, but that I don't matter enough for people to bother engaging with me at all.

Now my daughter attends Jewish summer camp, a different one from the ones I went to. I try not to impose my own camp experiences on her. To not compare. To not contrast. And to not force my own politics, my own wishes for the future, my own read of Israel and Palestine, on her newly emerging understanding of the place. Her camp runs programs on Israel. Seminars. Discussions. A delegation of Israeli counselors are brought over every year to inject the camp with a sense of Israel as an actual place. The camp leadership wants the campers to think of Israel as theirs.

One summer, on visiting day, I strike up a conversation with her sailing teacher. He is part of the Israeli delegation completing a year of national service in the Jewish community in Canada before enlisting in the IDF. "I've just returned from Israel," I tell him in Hebrew. "I was actually in Hebron, with Breaking the Silence."

I wait for a flicker of recognition, a bit of anti-occupation solidarity. I am testing him, I realize, and I hate myself for my own virtue-signaling. Still, I can't stop talking. "I write for *Haaretz*," I add, hoping for some affirmation that I belong to this joint Israeli-Diaspora community that he and I are both part of, via my daughter, at least for a summer. At least for this visiting day.

I tell him that I speak only Hebrew to my daughter, and that if he can please speak Hebrew to her during her next sailing lesson that would be great. I tell him Ill look for him on the international sailing competition rankings. "What's your last name again?" I shake his hand, this young Israeli who I hope sees me as a peer, as one of his own, but who isn't much older than my daughter and who probably doesn't read Haaretz, given that it's losing market share to the less liberal media. And it's in English anyway. Plus, he's only eighteen.

In a couple of years, my daughter's cohort will spend the summer in Israel, before returning to camp to work as counselors. But she hesitates about whether to join the Israel trip. She may prefer to travel somewhere else. Latin America. Asia. She may want to volunteer somewhere. Work on a social justice project. Get an additional high school course credit. But what she's really worried about, she tells me, is that I'll pepper her with political questions about the trip. About what they teach her. About the messages that circulate in their discussion sessions. About the occupation. About the Palestinians. Already she had been angry with me when I feigned puzzlement to her counselors, asking them what their *nikyaon sh'tachim* t-shirts mean. I knew enough to know it probably referred to the on-site camp volunteer clean-up crew. *Nikayon*: clean-up. *shetach*: territory or area. But I couldn't help remarking that the phrase also reminded me of the need to clean the Israeli *sh'tachim*, the word left-wing Israelis use to refer to the West Bank and Gaza, of the occupation. My daughter shot me a look. I tried to pivot back to small talk, asking her counselors what they were majoring in.

My kids know I've got plenty of opinions about Israel-Palestine. And they know I've been embroiled in Jewish community dynamics here in Ottawa. They know that several years ago, I came home late one night in tears after I was kicked out of a Jewish community fundraising dinner.

Following the talk, during book signing and handshaking, I had exchanged tense words with the organizers and the speaker about what I heard as a one-hour Islamophobic tirade coming from the stage. I told the speaker her speech was racist, delivering my message in Hebrew, since she had told the audience that she speaks Hebrew and that she absolutely loves Israel. After my outburst, I saw the organizer signal the security guards and a minute later I felt a hand on each of my elbows, leading me outside. I looked over at the owner of the right hand: my kids' swimming teacher. Apparently the lifeguards at the JCC had been pressed into service as security guards for the event, and I was being publicly humiliated.

My kids know that I was barred from what should have been, according to the bylaws and typical conventions, a normal succession from vice-president to president of a Jewish community board I had faithfully served. Donors didn't like my politics on Israel-Palestine and had threatened to walk if I took the helm.

My kids are probably fairly sympathetic to their parents, as most kids are, at first at least. But soon they will discover their own opinions. Their own politics. And they might not agree with mine. Or they might. Or they might not agree with my politics but they might agree I've been mistreated. Or they might agree with my politics but still feel the organizations acted fairly. Or the reverse. And they will probably agree, no matter what, that I struggle with finding the right audience for my shifting views of the day. There's a matrix waiting to be filled in, as their own ideas about the world continue to crystallize.

The Ottawa winter is finally giving way to spring, and I am strolling through my local park, taking advantage of the empty pond that the city drains each winter to make room for children on sleds. In early spring, after the snow has melted and the muddy pond floor is dry and exposed, and before the park forms a backdrop to the beds of tulips the city plants each spring, I am reminded of the kind of dry riverbed that Israelis and Palestinians call a *wadi*. Israel-Palestine—where the *wadis* are—is the place of my scholarly occupation, my preoccupation, my criticism, and my obsession. My attachment to Israel has been deep, nurturing, and complex—but it has come at an emotional cost.

I once thought I'd move to Israel permanently. Make aliyah. Become a Member of Knesset and a professor. Maybe become a diplomat. Negotiate for peace. I would live on a kibbutz and I'd commute to the cities as needed. Jerusalem for the Knesset. Jerusalem or Tel Aviv or Haifa or Beer Sheva for the university. I'd help bring peace to the Middle East while fulfilling my own private longings for rootedness and belonging.

Before our relationship began to fray, Israel seduced me, as it does so many Diaspora Jews. And as the country began to betray me, I felt the fallout within my relationship with others, here, in North America. In so many ways, Israel has been an instigator of, and a bystander to, the tension that has come to define so many Diaspora Jewish relationships. If we didn't have Israel, I suppose we'd have something else on which to place and measure our shifting, insecure identities.

So tonight, I'm living out the path I actually took. Tonight I stare at my eerily long shadow, the low light stretching my limbs until I look like an alien, while listening to a podcast on my iPhone. It's Michael Enright, a CBC journalist, interviewing the Israeli author David Grossman. Despite Grossman being a symbol of the Israeli peace movement, in his musings on this podcast, I glean a few lines of *hasbara*—the talking points that have come to dominate much of Jewish community and Israeli Jewish conversations about Israel. Grossman describes residing in a "violent, hateful, sometimes crazy area — we look and see what Arabs are doing to Arabs.... One can just imagine what they would have done to us if they had the power." He suggests the miserable living conditions of West Bank Palestinian refugees are a function of the Arab states' desire to "protest against Israel." Enright doesn't challenge him on his ethnic stereotyping. He doesn't press him to acknowledge how the Palestinians became refugees in the first place. Once I would have forgiven Grossman the erasure of this history, chalking it up to conciseness. But now I hear it as a symptom of a larger problem in Israel, a problem that infects the way so many in my community characterize the issues.

I used to think Grossman's way about the refugees. When I was twenty, and studying as an overseas student at the Hebrew University, trying to eke out fast and loose essays to leave more time for Thursday night falafel on Ben Yehuda Street and weekends at the kibbutz disco in the Negev, I wrote in a term paper that the Palestinians, including the refugees among them, had been "used by the Arab states as pawns." When my TA handed back the paper, I saw that he had awarded me a B- for my middling effort and had circled that phrase. "*How* were they used as pawns? Provide evidence; explain," he had written. I had no answer. It was my first lesson in the intellectual damage that talking points can do.

But there are also touching turns in that David Grossman interview, like when he calls himself a Jewish atheist who loves studying the Bible; or when he describes the revival of modern Hebrew—how the Bible didn't have the words for ice cream, crane, or helicopter, and so those terms had to be invented by Hebrew language pioneers like Eliezer Ben-Yehuda, who spoke only Hebrew to his child even when the modern version of the language barely existed; and when Grossman says that instead of living "in a fortress," he longs to "live in a home," and considers how we can all too easily become the victim of our own stories.

As I listen to the podcast, I am already on social media, casting about for words to capture what I think of the interview.

And then a familiar tension settles into my shoulders. No doubt there will be some virtue-signaling on my part, as I try to walk the line between being heard and respected by those critical of Israel and being accepted by the mainstream community. No doubt there will be some pushback from others—whether articulated or kept private.

"Israel is like my child," my baba once said to me. "It's hard for me to hear it being criticized." When she said that, I relaxed. "Thank you for admitting that, Baba. Now we can really talk."

In my Facebook post that night, I end up pointing out the *hasbara* I heard in the interview while also acknowledging the beautiful moments. I close my post by writing, "It's Israel, after all."

A couple of years later, I discover an Israeli podcast, which is also a taped daily drive-in morning show. A portion of every podcast involves a call-in segment. Today's topic: tell us something interesting about a house you once lived in. One man says he lived in a famous writer's house on the very first street in Rehovot. A woman talks about a grisly murder that had occurred in her apartment years before she moved in. "It's haunted," she says. And then a seventy-year-old woman named Galia phones in. "I lived in the Green House when I first moved to Israel as a baby," she says. "Ah, the Green House," the announcer replies. "That's the one in the Arab village of Shaykh Muwannis, where the Arab residents fled-slash-were-expelled."

"That's the one. We were so lucky they housed us there," she says, referring to the government task of housing new immigrants in the fifties. "It was such a sense of community. Neighborly feeling like you just don't see anymore, these days."

After her call, the announcers riff on "OK, boomer" for a bit, adding, "C'mon, now, folks in Israel in 2019 are still neighborly." They talk about how completely adorable she was and then move onto the next segment.

I visited the site of the Green House on my last visit to Tel Aviv, where it now functions as part of the Tel Aviv University campus. Eitan Bronstein, the founder of Zochrot, had taken me there one afternoon on a personal tour of three sets of ruins of Palestinian villages right in the midst of the vibrant Hebrew city of Tel Aviv. As we approached the nearby Palestinian cemetery, with tombstones still visible amidst the long grass and weeds that had grown up around them, Bronstein warned me not to take pictures in any other direction. There were security installations nearby. Sure enough, Israeli security personnel came out from a nearby building to ask us about our activities. We explained what we were doing and hoped they'd leave us be. But instead they led us down to a parking lot and detained us, holding on to our passports and IDs until they could verify with their supervisors that we posed no "security threat."

Because of that delay, I missed meeting my new baby cousin whose young father I had made plans with for my remaining hours in the city. The Nakba is not totally invisible, but it emerges in tiny specks of Israeli awareness, like fireflies, before disappearing again. One has to be willing to look for it, though, sometimes at the risk of being deemed a threat.

Those tiny specks of political and justice-based awareness jostle for my attention, amidst the care I must give to my personal and professional identity, to my role in the community, and to the domestic tasks I've let pile up. There are dishes and laundry and my husband who deserves a conversation about something other than the professional dynamics that keep me tightly wound. And there are my own son and daughter, who need and deserve some interaction that may be shaped by politics but isn't necessarily defined by it.

CHAPTER 14

Cancel Culture

2020

I'm awakened by the sound of tapping in quick succession. I try to deci-pher the source. It sounds like scurrying and it seems to be coming from inside the wall, inches from my pillow. Mice, I think. I roll over in bed and luxuriate in the high-thread-count linens I've been given while I visit my great-aunt in her mid-century modern home in Southern Cali-fornia. Deciding that my afternoon nap is over, I reach for my phone atop the nightstand. There's a text from a colleague in Canada. "Look at the RWJO Facebook feed," it says.

I had blocked the Canadian head of the far-right rogue group (RWJO—"right wing Jewish organization," I'll call it here) some time ago. The group's thuggish tactics—combined with the fact that some US civil rights organizations have deemed it a hate group—fills me with discomfort. I didn't want the group head following me and knowing my whereabouts. Google the group and images of middle-aged men in bomber jackets and sunglasses pop up. Other photos depict actual fistfights.

I follow my colleague's tip and scroll through the group's Facebook page. I see that the head of the group has been uploading video speeches about me: long, eerily calm tirades. I decide to unblock his personal page so I can continue to keep tabs. Poking around further, I see that others have been posting about me too. I'm not altogether surprised, since I'm on a panel event that has been recently announced. A Jewish Studies

© The Author(s) 2021

M. Sucharov, *Borders and Belonging: A Memoir,*

https://doi.org/10.1007/978-3-030-53732-6_14

center at a Canadian university has invited me to speak. The university was recently the site of a heated event and counterprotest on the topic of Israel-Palestine. Punches were thrown; rumors about what was or wasn't chanted by the competing groups had circulated with a vengeance. This upcoming panel—a few weeks from now—is meant to bring some arms-length analysis to the broader situation and I'm pleased to be on it.

I soon learn that more and more people have been calling the center to urge them to disinvite me.

But I'm too excited by my upcoming family vacation—I've just wrapped up a Jewish Studies conference in San Diego, and my husband and kids are about to join me in California—to have this attention cause me too much distress. And I'm curious to see what my friends and colleagues will say.

So I post about it on my Facebook page, and reactions come in swiftly. As expected, I get lots of support. Feeling emboldened, I decide to tag one of the people I'd seen on someone else's page encouraging folks to call the center to complain about my slated participation. He does not take kindly to the pile-on—against him, this time—that results.

"Block the RWJO head from all your accounts," an acquaintance tells me by private messenger. I thank him for his concern and explain my strategy of wanting to know what's being posted about me. Plus, as this saga unfolds, I've been trying to engage the RWJO head directly, in a closed Facebook group I find myself in with him. I'm probably naive in thinking about the old adage of using honey, rather than vinegar, to persuade. But anyway, I always claim I believe in engagement so I'm trying to stay consistent. I had joined this group for research purposes. Within our discussion thread, other colleagues—including ones I disagree with on the politics of Israel-Palestine—are thankfully telling him it would be a bad idea to get me canceled.

And then I alert the head of the Jewish Studies center, the one who had invited me. "I hope you will take steps to ensure my safety," I write, "now that the RWJO is involved with railing against me."

"Yikes," he replies. "The RWJO, huh?"

I email my close friends who live in that city. "I hope one or both of you can attend the event," I write. "Your support will mean a lot." I consider reaching out to some old camp friends I haven't seen in a long time, maybe trying to get them to come too. They'll surely want to protect me, I think, if things go awry. But maybe they will find my political perspective problematic and might even agree that I'm the wrong person for the panel. That would be awkward for them and for me. Probably best I don't.

Over the many years I've been an expert on the topic of Israel-Palestine, I've valued public engagement and have rarely turned down an invitation to speak to a broader audience. I've even written a book about the importance of scholars stepping into the public fray. But when it comes to Jewish community audiences, the reactions I've received have been mixed. Some audiences, of course, have seemed to appreciate my analytical lens, praising me for being "balanced." But not always.

There was the old family friend who reached out to me on Facebook— many years after we had seen each other in person—to invite me to come to his city to give a talk to the Jewish community. He met me, with my baby in tow, at the airport, and appeared to listen politely during my guest lecture. But the next day, he promptly unfriended me on social media.

There was the woman who stormed out of a living room talk I'd been invited to give by a local Jewish women's group. Driving across town in winter, I settled myself in a corner chair in the suburban living room and proceeded to lay out the scope of my talk. When I raised the topic of BDS as a subject for analysis—"This is what people are talking about," I said, "so it's useful for us to try to understand the dynamics of protest these days"—her eyes flashed: "I don't want to hear about boycotts. This is Israel we are talking about. Our country. How dare you."

And then there was the evening, several years before that, when I had been invited by a local Jewish organization to give some remarks about an Israeli film at a public community screening. It was a documentary about the longstanding political rivalry between Yitzhak Rabin and Shimon Peres. Rabin had been the more successful of the two, but had paid for that success with his life.

As the film concluded, I approached the podium, shuffled my notes, and proceeded to relay my best political science models of leadership and internal party dynamics. As a brand-new professor, I wanted to sound professional and scholarly. "This film portrays the idea of competitive leadership. Rabin and Peres were lifelong political rivals," I said. "Here are some frameworks we can use to put it all into context." I looked up from my notes and into the faces of the audience members, took a breath, and continued. "What's especially interesting is that while so much of Israeli political history has entailed clashing ideologies, here were two political giants who were actually from the same party."

"We don't want your pencils and your textbooks!" an older woman yelled from the front row. She had an Israeli accent.

I looked at her. "She's right," a woman sitting next to her said. "We just want to enjoy the film!"

My cheeks burned. I pictured throwing my notes on the floor and walking out. But I adjusted my microphone, grabbed the edges of the podium, and continued with my prepared remarks, avoiding their eyes.

A few days after that social media campaign to get me disinvited from the panel at the Canadian university, I receive another Facebook notification: someone has tagged me in a post that the center's director has sent around to the membership list:

We believe that there has been a misunderstanding among some community members about our panelists and the goals of this event. In particular, some community members have fixated on the supposed support for BDS on the part of one panelist, in spite of her having written in the Canadian Jewish News that "I have gone on record many times opposing the end game of BDS." Indeed, some have sought to protest and shut down the program as a whole. All three of our panelists are pro-Israel. While they may hold different views about how to achieve peace in the Middle East, this event is about the climate for Jews on university campuses, and what steps might be taken to address the issues they face.

My facial muscles tense. I know that the director is trying to engage in damage control. Image maintenance. Community relations. But I don't appreciate having my political credentials trotted out in an attempt to render me kosher. This is a scholarly center and I have been invited as a scholar-expert. Nothing beyond my credentials and my expertise and my analytical and communication skills, I think to myself, should be part of the decision to determine whether I am fit for speaking.

I write to the director: "Shouldn't we be focusing on scholarly contributions? We are stooping to their level, we're playing their game." Soon after, the director announces that the event will be postponed until they can get better security measures in place. Predictably, RWJO makes hay of it. They think they've successfully had me canceled.

And then a reporter for the Canadian Jewish News contacts me, looking for an interview. I offer him some quotes, which he takes:

"This is an academic event. It is sponsored by a university centre … I am a scholar who is active in publishing, speaking, writing and teaching in a Jewish studies context. And when a scholar is invited at the behest of a scholarly centre within a university, nothing more than scholarly credentials should be part of the public conversation as to whether someone should or shouldn't be part of a panel."

And:

"Open discourse within universities and the maintenance of academic freedom is a cornerstone of democracy. And so any attempted interference with that, and any buckling to such pressure, would be undermining the role and purpose of the university."

When the news piece comes out, I post it on my Facebook page. The piece includes more comments from the director, assuring the audience that I oppose BDS.

And then another colleague comments: "I didn't know you went on record as opposing BDS." I try to be quick on my feet. I don't want to deny anything I have written in the past: I stand by my writings intellectually, even if my views have shifted over time—it's a natural evolution I encourage my students to be open to, maybe to even embrace in their own careers. But I do want to take the opportunity to make a broader point. So I reply, "across hundreds of op-eds over the last decade my views about BDS (whether as tactic or as a set of political goals) have evolved. One can find various opinions among writers who think, write, grapple and question in an ongoing conversation with the writer's readers, if one wants to cherry pick a particular line to suit an agenda."

For that short comment, I get several "likes."

A few weeks later, the director tells me they've settled on a new date, far into the future. Only those who have been invited directly are to know the details. "Don't discuss it on social media," he says. I don't feel entirely comfortable with this new arrangement. There is something inimical to the scholarly enterprise to keeping a panel event a secret. Scholarly engagement is meant to be a public pursuit. I make my concerns known to the director quietly, and then I desist. I'm a guest, after all. And then, a few months later, the pandemic hits. "Can we move it to Zoom?" the director asks the panelists. "Sure," we reply. And then a month after that, the director cancels the event outright. "People's focus has shifted," he says. I don't reply.

One day, I receive an email from a Jewish group announcing the imminent start of the new Daf Yomi cycle. For the last century, clusters of Jews around the world have chosen to study one page of Talmud—the combination of the Mishna and Gemara and associated commentaries—per day. Every seven and a half years, the entire cycle starts anew. I'd heard about Ilana Kurshan's popular memoir tracing her own Daf Yomi journey, but I haven't ever seriously considered doing it. This short email is irresistible, though. I decide to jump in.

I immediately announce my intentions on Facebook, as I often do. It's a form of sharing, connection, and self-binding—sharing my goals publicly in hopes of maintaining my personal commitment. And then I decide to launch a Facebook group for the purpose. Soon I have a dozen members, then a hundred, then two hundred. My dad decides to join. "It'll be a good way to keep me healthy for the next seven and a half years," he writes.

A week or two later, a colleague who has joined the Daf Yomi group messages me. "I was thinking, I must ask you to join our workshop here at Cambridge University on religion and the university and the media. We could get you in and out real quick. Hope you will say yes!" I check the dates against my teaching schedule this term and take only a minute to decide. "I'd be delighted," I write.

I am reminded, as I so often am, that social media is a vehicle for alienation and mistrust, for hardened positions and cancel culture, and also for community and connection, for mutual exploration and discovery. So I write up the episode of my having almost gotten canceled by the right-wing Jewish organization as an essay for Cambridge workshop. There, I am wined and dined and given a tour of the college's dining hall and the pantry where faculty fellows can cellar their wine, and where I have an opportunity to discuss and parse the dynamics of public engagement and scholarly activism astride the quad—where, my husband reminds me, the Great Court Run scene in his favorite movie, *Chariots of Fire*, is set.

There was a time when I actively opposed BDS—both its endgame of calling for refugee return, and its academic boycott tactic. I believed that refugee return spelled the end of the Jewish State, and that Israel had the right to define its core identity. As for academic boycotts, I believed them to be altogether unethical and against the fundamental spirit of scholarly exchange. I soon became one of the busiest bloggers on the Open Zion blog on the Daily Beast—an outlet created by liberal Zionist commentator Peter Beinart, where I challenged pro-BDS positions from a liberal standpoint. When the outlet finally closed, I called my parting piece "No one loves a liberal Zionist."

And while I do not currently personally embrace BDS, I'm now much more ambivalent about the ethics of academic boycotts, rather than opposing them outright. I no longer feel comfortable actively standing in the way of those advocating for BDS. As a non-violent struggle, it's a legitimate means, I suppose, for the Palestine solidarity movement to draw attention to the fundamental human rights issues and patterns of oppression that define what others prefer to call "the conflict." And as for refugee return—the most controversial of the three BDS "pillars" because it would threaten the idea of a Jewish majority, something Israeli state identity is predicated on—I was moved by the words of a Palestinian Israeli Member of Knesset a few years ago. When asked by a participant at an evening salon event in Ottawa, "How will the Palestinians be persuaded to give up their right of return?" he responded simply, "Why should they?" My mind was transported to Palestinian houses and olive groves. To the Palestinian desire for home. It's a longing that should be familiar to Zionists everywhere: collective memory is a powerful thing, and perhaps dual return—a dual national homeland where both sets of histories, memories, languages, and cultures are upheld—is the most just option.

Not being able to determine whether I'm for or against BDS—since I've been deliberately oblique about my position on that issue in my public writings over the last couple of years—the RWJO's head settled on calling me a "BDS enabler." I smiled slightly when I read that. That label was pretty fair in its nuance; I have to give him that.

As for the mice in the walls that woke me from my nap that day in Southern California, my great-aunt later explained to me, after I inquired delicately, that the sound was not rodents at all. It was olives cascading down from the tree outside my window.

CHAPTER 15

Dreams

2020

I'm walking to campus to teach my morning class. With my earbuds in,
I'm listening to an investigative podcast about Bill Cosby's monstrous
deeds. Having gotten a few pages of memoir edits in before leaving the
house, I didn't have much time for breakfast so I took my daily anti-
anxiety medication on a partially empty stomach. The two clementines
plus a piece of toast with pumpkin-seed butter wasn't enough, apparently,
to stave off nausea. As I walk up the stairs toward my classroom, I feel
nauseated and overheated. And now a wave of panic descends: maybe
the nausea is something worse, I think. I realize this is just my usual
anxiety tricks and I'm able to talk it down through practiced mindfulness
techniques. The panic subsides, or so I believe, but the nausea remains. I
enter the classroom and face my waiting students.

"Wellness is one of my beats," I begin. "I have developed teaching
philosophies about teaching to the whole student. Now you are seeing
what it means to be a whole teacher. I'll cut to the chase. I'm nauseated.
I feel like shit. Please get into pairs and talk about your op-ed pitches due
next class, while I step out for five minutes. I'll be back soon."

I step into the hallway and find a seat next to the expansive windows.
I look down at the rushing winter river and manage to collect myself.

"I guess I'm having a weird morning," I say when I return to the
classroom. "I was listening to a podcast about Bill Cosby on the way
here. Man, he was a monster. How many of you grew up on reruns of

The Cosby Show?" Two students raise their hands. "I'm a child of the eighties," I say, "so *The Cosby Show* was huge. There are the critiques of its use of color-blindness, but for me, being a white kid, the biggest impact wasn't the racial aspect, but its depiction of an intact family. As a child of divorce—" my voice cracks. I try to finish my sentence, but now, suddenly, I am sobbing. "I'm sorry," I say, through tears, "it's just ..." And now I am heading out of the room again, telling my students, "talk amongst yourselves, I need to take another moment."

I find another seat outside the room, this one closer to the classroom door. I cover my face with my hands as the tears flow. My shoulders are heaving.

I look up as one of my students takes a seat next to me. "Tell me to leave at any point," she says, her eyes wide and kind. "But I couldn't just let you sit here all by yourself."

"Thank you," I say, through tears.

She tells me that she also experiences anxiety and proceeds to lead me through a sensory grounding exercise.

"Focus on your breath," she says. "Can you hear three sounds?" I nod. "Now feel the ground beneath your feet. Now feel the chair underneath you." I nod again. "Now take three deep breaths." I comply.

"Thank you," I say again. I explain, my voice still shaky, that my usual anxiety is panic about an allergy attack. But this time it's more brute emotion. This time, it's different. "I don't quite get it." My words are muffled by my crying.

Soon, I gather myself and we walk back into the class to the students' waiting faces, etched with concern.

I take a deep breath and manage to lead a lively enough discussion about pitches and op-eds and what happens if you write a piece that creates the kind of blowback Mayim Bialik experienced when her op-ed about Harvey Weinstein and the casting couch and "conservative choices" as well as her unusual "nose" and "chin," led to a backlash she did not expect. It's one of my favorite op-eds to teach. I relish uncovering the reason for the blowback: her argument was answering a different question than the implicit question she posed at the beginning of the piece.

At the end of class, another student, who I've taught before, follows me out. "I just wanted to see how you're doing," he says.

"Yeah, better, thank you. Hey, you had me last term," I say. "Nothing like this ever happened then. It's really weird, huh?"

"It's not weird at all," he says. "It's human."

Lately, I've been having a series of recurring dreams about Jason, my longtime friend from camp. The dreams always include a mix of pleasant feelings and waves of guilt. In the dream, Jason and I are wrapped in a warm embrace while I struggle to figure out how this intimacy will impact my current, stable marriage, the life I have consciously built and am grateful for. Waking up from the dream feeling unmoored, I will these dreams to go away. And yet they return.

When I walked into the engagement party our families put on for Steve and me many years ago, I burst into tears. It was an afternoon garden gathering at the gracious home of my aunt. It was not a surprise; we had even helped a little in the planning. But walking into the kitchen, where Steve's mom was sprinkling parsley over platters of homemade hummus, and my mom, stepmom, and aunt were tending to the desserts and drinks, a wave of emotion overtook me. *I don't deserve this happiness; I wasn't raised for this stability*, I thought. Bewildered, my mom took me into the book-lined den and helped me gather myself so I could greet guests and pose for pictures. I was wearing a black summer dress embroidered with tiny flowers and he was wearing a linen shirt from Banana Republic in a shade of slate blue that was popular that season.

I know full well what Jason represents: a time that was more precarious on a familial level, with my parents' breakup and my childhood filled with episodes of uncertainty and threat. A time when I was entering adolescence—he called me Sooch, in the style of nickname that made me feel I was invited to be one of the boys, just as I was also the girl he had always liked *in that way*, as he later confessed, when we actually found ourselves locked in a moment of physical intimacy some years later. A time when I was ensconced in the Jewish community and felt buoyed by my connection to Israel in a way that felt less complicated than it would later turn out to feel.

It was a time when my doubts did not extend to the politics around Israel-Palestine; when I didn't have to prove to the community whether I am kosher or treyf; when I didn't have to randomly search for social capital in contradictory corners; when my main goal was to impress my teachers and my counselors with my Hebrew, my singing, my acting, and my *ruach*. All those authority figures set the same standards: be smart, be talented, and be committed.

Any intellectual or philosophical conflicts I did experience when I was young, wrapped up in the expansive arms of the Jewish community, had involved the usual questions about God and belief. *Why do we have to pray out loud with our teachers patrolling the aisles? Prayer is something that should be private, and should be done only if one feels moved to do so. And what do you mean God wrote the Bible? That is simply not possible.* My sixth grade teachers, not able to cope with my challenges, would send me down the hall, to the Jewish high school adjacent to the elementary wing, to have a discussion with the head rabbi. Smiling at me across the table in his study lined with Judaic texts, the rabbi was patient with my interrogations. And even as I verbally sparred with him, energized by the debate, I knew that this tight-knit community was nourishing me. Far from wanting to turn my back on it, I cherished being a part of it.

By twelfth grade, when I had already been living in Vancouver for five years, Jason and some other friends invited me back to Winnipeg to perform in their song festival entry at the citywide Jewish high school event. Having entered a maudlin song in sixth grade, before moving away from Winnipeg, I was thrilled at the opportunity to perform again, this time with a more sophisticated entry. But during rehearsal, the organizing teacher—the one who taught Jason and me in fifth grade, the one who had been the subject of our inside jokes that were a blend of mocking and reverence—forbade me from joining. Since I no longer lived in Winnipeg, I was ineligible to perform, he said. That was the second time this teacher made me cry.

"After everything I've done for this community," I said as I wept, wiping my eyes on my sleeve. "Years of Jewish day school, a decade of Jewish camp." It was a fit of hyperbole on my part, of course. I had forgotten how things actually work: who builds the institutions and who gets served by them. What I really meant to say was, *This community anchors me. Please don't leave me to float away.*

In the end, I was permitted to join the performance on the condition that I did not sing; I would be allowed to tap a tambourine against my palm. I stood on the stage in my tapered Levi's and a favorite shirt, my lips not moving, feeling betwixt and between.

And maybe this was why, after organizing but before attending a standing-room-only panel on the topic of "Jewish Politics" at a recent conference, I got distracted. As I approached the seminar room in the crowded hotel, I spotted one of my counselors from Jewish day camp four decades earlier. He was tall and lanky and I recall him entertaining us on the daily bus ride to the campsite where we learned the difference between kindling and tinder. As conference-goers shuffled by us, we stood there, reminiscing about Jewish Winnipeg of the seventies. It was only when I entered the conference room, climbed over people strewn in the aisles, and took my seat at the front as the moderator introduced me, that I realized I was late to my own session.

I recently had a chance to see Jason, after many years, during a chance meeting in Winnipeg at a Bar Mitzvah. We sat, along with another old camp friend, in the same hall where that song festival had taken place almost thirty years earlier. As the staff cleaned up around us, the three of us sat and reminisced—about school, friends, teachers, and our families—until late. "It was great to catch up," he wrote me later. "I could have gone on all night."

Mark, the counselor who wrote my letters after camp, sometimes crosses paths with me on Facebook. But whatever mutual admiration we had when I was a teen at camp and he was my counselor is now weighed down by the strains of Israeli-Palestinian politics, and we duke this out on social media, not always charitably. I'm still grateful to him for helping introduce me to Israeli pop music culture and instilling in me a love of spoken Hebrew, throughout the years of Hebrew summer camp. Our tensions are a reminder that a sense of common cultural connection can lead to different political conclusions, and very different conceptions of what justice entails.

Jabir's profile on Facebook pops up now and again when I look for him out of curiosity; he still, all these years after our short relationship at McGill and afterward, has the same handsome face and penetrating eyes. In his profile picture, he is surrounded by a lovely family of his own. I send him a "friend" request. When he doesn't respond, I'm torn between disappointment and relief.

As for Oded, my friend and colleague from Jerusalem, we plan to catch up in person this spring, where we will both be attending a large international relations conference. Last time we saw each other at one of these meetings, in New Orleans, we talked about families and relationships over vegan rice bowls. A year earlier, we had walked along the snowy sidewalks of Toronto and talked about Israeli politics. This time, in Honolulu, there will be sun and sand and ocean and palm trees, and Oded will bring his teenage son from Jerusalem. I might ask his son, who I will finally get to meet, how he feels about going into the Israeli army—or I might not.

CPSIA information can be obtained
at www.ICGtesting.com
Printed in the USA
LVHW080206121020
668558LV00011B/182